THE
PERFECT DAY
FORMULA

HOW TO OWN THE DAY
AND CONTROL YOUR LIFE

CRAIG BALLANTYNE

THE PERFECT DAY FORMULA

How to Own the Day and Control Your Life

ISBN 978-1-61961-355-3

PRAISE FOR THE PERFECT DAY FORMULA

"Everybody wants to live the perfect life but fail to understand you do that by designing and living the perfect day, day after day. This book shows you exactly what you have to do to create that day."

– LARRY WINGET, SIX TIME NYT/WSJ BESTSELLING AUTHOR OF GROW A PAIR, SOCIAL COMMENTATOR AND TELEVISION PERSONALITY

"Craig Ballantyne was the first person to push me on the importance of creating my Perfect Day—a habit that is the secret behind all of my accomplishments. He is always an inspiration. As a busy mom of two young kids, I strongly believe this book is required reading if you wish to accomplish something big!"

– DIANA KEUILIAN, AUTHOR OF THE RECIPE HACKER

"Like his site Early To Rise, Craig's book relies on ancient wisdom and classic thinkers—including my favorite, the Stoics—to help you organize your day and run your life."

– RYAN HOLIDAY, AUTHOR OF THE OBSTACLE IS THE WAY

"Before implementing Craig's easy to use principles, I was always begging for more time. Running a 7-figure business was not just taking over my ability to take care of my health, but was taking up any time I was able to spend with my husband and kids. That was until Craig came to the rescue. Using Craig's Perfect Day Formula I am now able to successfully run and grow my business, have time to exercise and eat healthy every day, and end my work day at 3pm to spend the rest of the afternoon with my husband and kids. Thank you Craig for showing me that life can be filled with Perfect Days!"

– ISABEL DE LOS RIOS, AUTHOR AND CO-FOUNDER OF BEYONDDIET.COM

"This is a good, smart book about—not just personal productivity—but also achievement and balance and happiness in life. Craig's approach is, like all good approaches, both personal and universal. I will recommend this to friends and colleagues."

– MARK FORD, FOUNDER, EARLYTORISE.COM

"A success masterpiece! I've been studying the author's teachings through his daily online publication for years now so I was excited to see that he has taken his hard-earned wisdom and shared it with the world in the form of this book. Craig comes from humble beginnings but rather than use that as an excuse, he made a decision to learn the correct philosophies, strategies and action steps to attain both personal and business success. Utilize his Perfect Day formula for controlling what YOU can control and expect to live a life in which you are healthier, wealthier, wiser, and above all, happier than you might ever have expected you could be!"

– BOB BURG, CO-AUTHOR OF THE GO-GIVER

"Craig's idea of having a 'not-to-do list' created a powerful, lasting improvement in my productivity. Craig's mastery of critical life skills is one of the many reasons why I invite him to speak at my youth entrepreneurship events each year."

– SIMON BLACK, SOVEREIGNACADEMY.ORG

"It might feel like a stretch to imagine having a perfect day, but when you learn how to master the ideas Craig shares in his new book and you focus on what really matters, you'll be able to make better decisions, achieve your goals and create the life you want."

– JOE POLISH, GENIUS NETWORK

"Craig is the king of owning his day and the master of teaching you how to do the same. His authentic message comes as by-product of years of 'in-the-trenches' experience that brought him to the pinnacle of success—and the opportunity is now yours to have. You owe it to yourself to read this book and experience a lifetime of freedom!"

– BEDROS KEUILIAN, FOUNDER OF FIT BODY BOOT CAMP FRANCHISE

"As the saying goes "any day above ground is a good day" – so why not cherish this gift and make it a great day. It takes just a few simple routines like those Craig shares to set you and your life free."

– VERNE HARNISH, FOUNDER OF ENTREPRENEURS' ORGANIZATION
AND AUTHOR OF SCALING UP (ROCKEFELLER HABITS 2.0)

"Craig's manual shows you how to design your life, by breaking it down into the smallest unit—controlling and

designing each day. Step one: Create the perfect day. Step two: Live it. Step three: Repeat until you're living your perfect life."

– ALWYN COSGROVE, CO-AUTHOR OF THE NEW RULES OF LIFTING SERIES

"The Perfect Day Formula is the guide you need to regain your most prized asset: freedom. My wife and I are busy entrepreneurs with 5 children. His teachings provided us with more structure, more freedom, and we finally retook ownership of our lives. A must-read for anyone interested in having a better life."

– CHEF GUI ALINAT, AUTHOR OF THE CHEF'S REPERTOIRE

"Big dreams don't come true on their own, and legends aren't born—they're built one day and one decision at a time. Craig Ballantyne is an architect at creating success, and this book is your blueprint."

– RYAN MURDOCK, AUTHOR OF VAGABOND DREAMS AND PERSONAL FREEDOM, CO-FOUNDER OF SHAPESHIFTER MEDIA, INC.

"This book is a MUST READ & FOLLOW. I am living proof that when you follow the steps in The Perfect Day Formula you will transform your life. Before I had the Perfect Day Formula, I never felt like I had complete control over my day. Instead, I felt like my day controlled me. As entrepreneur with multiple companies and two small children, being able to 'get it all done' while staying focused and present is essential to my success and well being. I am forever grateful that I learned the Perfect Day Formula from Craig and credit my morning magic time to my rapid success."

– LORI KENNEDY, FOUNDER OF THE WELLNESS BUSINESS ACADEMY

"Wow! What a book. If you want to not just get through the day, but seize the day this book is a must-read. Craig gives you a step by step blueprint that goes beyond tired time management techniques and shows you how to live a life of joy and fulfillment."

– DAVE DEE, "THE KING OF ONE TO MANY SELLING"
AND CHIEF MARKETING OFFICER, GKIC

CONTENTS

THE PERFECT DAY

"First say to yourself what you would be; and then do what you have to do."

— EPICTETUS

Imagine for a moment what a perfect day would look like for you. Picture the most productive day you've ever had, and then imagine having that *every* day. For most of us, our perfect day is one where the tasks we accomplish are about more than just getting through the day, but rather about moving ahead in dramatic leaps and bounds toward our big goals and dreams.

It might be hard to imagine in your current state of affairs. But try. Take a leap of faith and visualize what such a day would look like.

On this hypothetical perfect day, what time would you get up? What would be the first and most important thing you do? How would your morning go? What would you do—and not do—after lunch? What time would you get home to your family? What would the atmosphere and conversation be like around the dinner table? What would you do in the evening hours as you reflect back on this perfect day? And what would be the last thing you do before you drift off to sleep?

Again, it may feel like a stretch to imagine such a day now. But most of us have, at least on occasion, experienced bits and pieces of a perfect day and wondered what it would be like to have that sensation all the time.

You know what I'm talking about. Often, it happens like this: For whatever reason, you wake up earlier than usual and get out of bed. It's a workday, so you either get a head start at home or go into the office long before everyone else arrives. As you start your work, free of distraction, you find it easier to quickly enter your "flow." Thirty minutes, an hour, maybe even two hours fly by with you barely noticing.

Eventually, there is a knock on your door or the telephone rings. The world has finally entered the race for the day, but you're so far ahead that nobody will ever catch you. The rest of your day goes smoothly, almost unbelievably so. At quitting time you feel a sense of accomplishment unlike any other day in recent memory and you have the entire night free to do whatever you want: spend time with your family, relax with a hobby, or visit friends.

Wow, you think. *Why can't every day be like this?*

It can.

But if you get up the next day at your normal time expecting to replicate your success, you will be disappointed. Your day will start with obstacles immediately thrown in your way, from family matters around the breakfast table to your phone buzzing with alerts of work emergencies.

Where did the magic of yesterday go? you wonder. For the rest of the day you find yourself playing catch-up to the world rather than the other way around. The official end of the workday can't come fast enough. And even when it finally arrives, you know your misery is not over. There is still a lot to do. It looks like you'll be canceling your evening plans and spending another hour, two, or three finishing up because you're running so far behind on your to-do list. This is the dreaded hamster wheel that we've all been stuck on.

Why is it that one day can be so different than the next? It's not just luck. The difference comes down to being proactive rather than reactive, and following a proven formula for success, one that requires implementing rules for your life, the 5 Pillars of Success, and the vision for your future. Don't worry if these sound new or intimidating. You will soon know how to use these tools to win your mornings—and own your days. In the process, you will win back your life.

In this book, I put forth a formula for what I call the **Perfect Day**. It's a formula based on focusing on the things you *can* control and taking action, every single day, to create the good life for yourself, as you define it.

By following this formula and taking this new approach to your daily life, you will not only reduce stress and anxiety and become more productive—but also find more time and energy to devote to the things that really matter to you, such as your family, friends, and hobbies.

The formula has its origins in a far corner of the ancient Roman Empire, where a wise man contemplated the true meaning of a "good life." His name was Epictetus and he was a teacher of an influential philosophy known as Stoicism.

Stoicism concerns itself with what it means to lead a good, moral, and productive life. This school of thought (and Epictetus himself) is over 2,000 years old, but the message behind it is timeless and universal. It speaks to anyone who struggles with the chaos of life.

As editor of the popular success website Early to Rise (ETR), I see firsthand how our readers struggle to push through the overwhelming grind of life and to keep some semblance of order and balance as they go through their busy days.

How can we find the true happiness, freedom, and success we're all looking for when we can hardly even keep up with our daily to-do lists? According to Epictetus, it all comes down to a fundamental distinction between the things we can control and those we cannot.

You probably have heard this before, or some variation of it. Epictetus's influence is all around us. For example, the Serenity Prayer used at Alcoholics Anonymous meetings comes from the philosopher's famous *Discourses*. It reads: "What, then, is to be done? To make the best of what is in our power, and take the rest as it naturally happens."

There is no value in worrying, being anxious, or wasting energy thinking about all the things we cannot influence. It does not serve you. We can't control whether someone else is wealthier, prettier, or happier than we are. But we *can* control how we act and, crucially, how we choose to spend our days. The good news is that you have a lot more control over your life—and happiness—than you might think.

Through the wisdom of the ages, you will find the happiness, freedom, and success you seek.

I look forward to hearing your success story.

To your Perfect Day,

Craig Ballantyne

Craig@Godfather.com

THE FORMULA

"It's time to stop being vague. If you wish to be an extraordinary person, if you wish to be wise, then you should explicitly identify the kind of person you aspire to become. If you have a daybook, write down who you're trying to be, so that you can refer to this self-definition. Precisely describe the demeanor you want to adopt so that you may preserve it when you are by yourself or with other people."

— EPICTETUS, ART OF LIVING

The wisdom of Epictetus, passed down over centuries, works just as well for you today as it did for ancient noblemen and emperors. Stoicism is a practical approach to a meaningful life, one of virtue and goodness, and to becoming your best self through continual, neverending improvement.

This philosophy teaches you to eliminate stress and guilt, and to ultimately lead a fulfilled life—one of joy, happiness, and inner peace rather than fear and regret. It helps you carry on in the face of adversity, prepares you for loss, and tempers your unhealthy desires.

Epictetus recognized that our insecurities toward external situations create an abundance of unhappiness. What upsets us, he said, are not things themselves but rather our judgments about those things. This is a common problem today. We spend too much time and energy comparing ourselves to others, which leads to pain and frustration.

For Epictetus, the solution was to focus instead on how you live your own life and spend your time. Born a slave, he rose to be a respected philosopher by following his formula. He teaches us to create boundaries, to eliminate envy and temptation, and to concentrate on what is right and meaningful for your best life.

This book is not just a set of inspiring principles but a concrete, daily *formula* for controlling your day, overcoming the chaos brought by others, and planning ahead to act proactively rather than reactively so that we can concentrate on what really matters in our lives.

When you apply these secrets to your daily routines, you will put into place a simple system that will lead to a better tomorrow, and you will see progress almost immediately. You will come to live a happy, virtuous, and fulfilled life, one governed by freedom rather than regret.

The formula for the Perfect Day is built on the Three Cs: Control, Conquer, and Concentrate.

Through the Perfect Day formula, we simply apply the Three Cs—Control, Conquer, and Concentrate—to different parts of the day. It looks like this:

It doesn't matter if you're single or married, if you have one child or five, if you're a freelance writer or a CEO, a shift worker or 9-to-5er, at the bottom of the corporate ladder or a soon-to-be retiree. The beauty of the Perfect Day formula is that it works for all of us.

When you use the Perfect Day system, breakthroughs will come. You will experience faster results than ever. You will succeed at work, climbing the ranks in your career, making more money, and generating more wealth and power.

Not only that, but you will have more energy and greater health; you will be happier; and most importantly, you'll have more freedom and time to give to your family, friends, and hobbies.

There is just one catch. The Perfect Day formula requires you to think differently and let go of your old ways. The average approach to life is not working for you or anyone else. Greatness requires you to think and act differently, especially in the face of intense peer pressure.

Be prepared to use the solutions in this book to summon up

strength you didn't know you possessed and to overcome all obstacles in the way of your Perfect Day.

It's okay if yesterday wasn't perfect. Or the day before. That's why you're reading this book. The mistakes of your past have taught you the lessons you need to create the solutions for your life. You can't change the past. No more regrets. It's time to focus on the future. In doing so, you must remember this mantra: Control your mornings. Conquer the chaos of your afternoons. Concentrate on what really matters in the evenings.

In the following chapters, you'll see exactly what I mean. But before we dive in to the step-by-step plan for having the Perfect Day, we need to introduce an underlying principle that is crucial to understanding the formula. It requires you to accept a strange but powerful paradox:

Structure = Freedom

This may sound odd, and you may bristle at the thought of more structure in your life, but very soon you'll come to see how more structure, created by having a set of rules for your life, liberates you and allows you to achieve your big goals and dreams.

Maybe your wish is to travel the world. To do so, you need more money and more time. Developing these resources starts with putting more structure in your days so that you can be more productive.

Or maybe your dream is to have more time to attend your children's games and recitals. Again, the answer lies in creating a more structured day so that you have more freedom at night.

Or perhaps your goal is to find true love. That requires a structured approach and commitment. Like any objective in life, it's not something you can pursue haphazardly.

Creating structure—by developing what I call the rules for your life—is the most important step in becoming more productive and less stressed. Structure is essential to earning your freedom. Your rules will lead you out of temptation, help you make the right decisions instinctively, and fuel your willpower to deal with the chaos of the day.

Your rules don't just help you get more done. They are also the foundation of more peaceful and loving interaction with your family and friends, more health and energy, and more overall contentment and peace of mind.

These rules will work for you no matter what your specific situation or circumstances. They work as well in modern-day New York or Los Angeles or Tokyo or Mumbai as they did in ancient Rome. They work well for the stockbroker, the writer, the factory worker, the office manager, and the student of philosophy. They work for today's rich and poor, just as they did for history's emperors, gladiators, and slaves alike.

Best of all, the rules you create for yourself with the Perfect Day formula won't require you to work harder than you work now. In fact, the opposite is true. You'll get more done in less time, and still make it home for dinner. You'll get more sleep and become a happier person.

Whatever the changes you wish to make—losing weight, improving your relationships, or making more money—I guarantee that adding more structure in your life will help get you there.

The Perfect Day formula not only creates good habits but it helps you get rid of vices in just a few days. When you eliminate bad habits, it becomes much easier to stick to good ones, which in turn allows you to make better decisions and secure faster results.

I know this from experience. I've spent my life researching how to have the perfectly productive day, compiling everything that has worked for my students, my readers, and me.

Who am I?

My name is Craig Ballantyne. I was the first to bring short burst workouts to the mass markets, setting off a fitness revolution, and the first to teach my peers the business systems for turning their ideas into an information product that could help thousands—and even millions—of people around the world.

My career began in 2000 when I started writing for *Men's Health* magazine at the age of 25. In 2001 I created what would eventually become one of the best selling fitness programs on the Internet (Turbulence Training), and so far have transformed the lives of over 175,000 people. Since 2008, my business clients have sold $175 million worth of health, fitness, and nutrition products. Today I have achieved my dream of running a thriving business (thanks to a step-by-step instructional story I'll share with you later) all while traveling the world (I've visited over 35 countries) and getting closer to my vision every day.

I don't say all this to brag but to show you that I walk the walk and can help you transform your life. I know because I've done it before. But I could not have done all these things without first conquering my own procrastination, personality, and time management demons using the Three C formula.

I learned everything the hard way so that you don't have to. I spent years as a struggling personal trainer, suffering from debilitating anxiety attacks, until I discovered how to control my mornings and win my days.

Along the way I have helped many men and women implement this system. Today I'm happy and free from anxiety, and I'm financially secure.

I'm not perfect, by any means. The journey is neverending. We all have areas for improvement, myself included, and I'll never stop my pursuit of getting better and overcoming my vices.

As a young man I was often anxious, angry, and jealous. I searched everywhere for advice and solutions for my weaknesses. I read hundreds of books, countless research studies, and thousands of magazine articles. I studied human physiology and psychology in both the formal academic world and through interviewing experts in human performance.

This book is a summary of what has worked from my decades-long journey of personal experiments in self-improvement. I discovered a system that has not only worked for me but has also helped my clients all over the world to lose weight, make more money, and find the loves of their lives. It will also work for you.

If you are like I once was, if you feel lost and frustrated by the chaos of the world today, don't let another minute pass you by. It's time to win back control of your life and get the freedom you deserve.

PART I

CONTROL THE MORNING

ONE

THE EPIC BATTLE FOR YOUR LIFE

"Discipline and freedom are not mutually exclusive but mutually dependent because otherwise, you'd sink into chaos."

– PAULO COELHO

Imagine Joe, an average guy with a regular office job. His day starts with waking up to an alarm. He hits the snooze button two, sometimes three or four times, leaving him late for work. He doesn't have time for breakfast at home so he grabs a large coffee—with plenty of sugar—and a donut on the way to the office. He barely makes it in on time—if he's lucky.

He starts work without a plan and wastes an hour just getting organized. He's hungry because he skipped breakfast. Lunch ends up being a trip to a fast food restaurant. At 2 p.m. he's nodding off in his chair.

The next thing Joe knows, it's almost 4 p.m. and he still has three hours of work to get done. There's no way that he'll be able to leave on time. It's only in this last mad dash under a deadline that he's finally able to get a few priorities completed, but he is never able to finish his to-do list because of the chaos of his day.

Looks like another late night is in his future. He phones home to let his family know the bad news. He won't be able to attend little Joe's ballgame, and he'll be late for daughter Katie's dance recital...but he'll try to make it for the end. Rushing out of the office at 7:30 p.m. he arrives just as the crowd launches into applause. Joe threw away his chance at freedom because his day lacked structure. Another day wasted because it started with chaos, not with control.

Now compare Joe's life to John, the CEO who knows how to have the Perfect Day.

John spent last night getting to bed on time thanks to his rules. He sleeps well and wakes up five minutes before his alarm clock goes off. His number one priority at work is managing his team, so he uses the first thirty minutes of his day preparing to run effective meetings.

He exercises and eats a healthy breakfast before heading into the office well prepared for his first appointment. He is on time and energized, not stressed. His day is scripted. Meetings are focused. Projects are finished before their deadlines.

He wraps up on time and makes it home for his kid's activities, time with his spouse, and he even has fifteen minutes for himself that he can spend in prayer, meditation, or gratitude.

John is free. Joe is not. Why? John is structured. Joe is not. John has rules. Joe has none. John is successful. Joe is lost.

If you've had the privilege to experience both sets of days, surely you'd pick John's results. This is the epic battle for your life. This is what the Perfect Day formula is all about.

TWO

HOW TO CONTROL YOUR DAYS

When my father passed away in the fall of 2008, I was reminded of the power of rituals and routines.

It all started in high school. Each afternoon when I'd come home I'd head up to my bedroom to change my clothes for my after school job. Before turning left into my room at the top of the stairs, I'd make a detour to my parents' bedroom on the right, where I'd inspect my father's nightstand for left-over candy. At night while watching television he'd snack on potato chips, chocolate bars, licorice, and other treats. It was like having a convenience store in our house. Thank goodness both he and I lived very active lives and had a fast metabolism to burn off all the calories.

This habit continued after I went off to college. When I'd return home during school breaks, I'd head up to my room to drop off my bags, and I'd make that right-hand turn at the top of the stairs to visit my father's candy shop.

After his funeral, I spent weekends visiting my mother to help sort through his affairs. During each visit I'd inevitably go up to my old room, and for months after his death I continued to make that right-hand turn. Alas, the candy shop was gone, but the old habit was hard to break.

As you can see, rituals are powerful. We must harness them for good and create the habits we need to control our days and win our mornings, and to put them in place for productivity and progress in life. The right rituals and routines make the right actions automatic, no matter how chaotic things get.

I learned this from Epictetus. He teaches us to control what you can, and cope with what you can't. Think about how this applies to your own life.

If your spouse or boss gets upset, there is no switch to turn them off.

If clouds gather and it starts to rain, you cannot wave the showers away.

You can't control the external world.

But you can control your thoughts, words, and deeds. When you do this, you can do remarkable things. You can write books, build companies, find the love of your life, lose weight, improve your health, and grow your wealth.

It all starts with recognizing what is under your control.

You can control what time you wake up, what habits you start the day with, what temptations enter your life, and what systems you have in place for dealing with those.

You can control your belief in yourself. You can take more control over your schedule and energy than you might believe right now. And most importantly, you can control your morning and in doing so, win your day.

The most important ritual in your life is what time you choose to get out of bed, and the best decision you can make is to start getting up fifteen minutes earlier. This will allow you to attack your number one priority first thing in the morning. Do not linger under the warm covers. That is for average people stuck in the struggles of ordinary lives. You are destined for greatness. You will not stand for failure.

Heed the most important lesson of this book: You control your behavior. Your success is your personal responsibility. Take action. Do the first things first. Do what matters even if you don't feel like it. Get up and give your number one priority the focus it deserves for at least fifteen minutes every morning.

But what if you're not a morning person, you ask? I get it. There is something romantic about being a night owl. But if you look at the great authors, artists, inventors...what do you find? You may be surprised, but the common thread is that they got their best work done in the morning.

The German writer Goethe, for example, wrote that the morning was when he felt "revived and strengthened by sleep and not yet harassed by the absurd trivialities of everyday life."

Victor Hugo, the author of *Les Miserables* and *The Hunchback of Notre Dame*, rose at sunrise, drank his morning coffee, ate two raw eggs, and then wrote until 11 a.m.

Beethoven, Schubert, and Mahler woke at dawn and composed until early afternoon.

Van Gogh began painting at seven in the morning.

The great architect Frank Lloyd Wright did his sketches between 4 a.m. and 7 a.m.

Dickens and Darwin did their best writing in the morning before taking long walks in the afternoon to fuel their creativity. And Hemingway, no matter how much he drank the night before, knew that it was best to write after the sun's first light.

Even Stephen King, the American horror master, writes his chilling tales before noon.

Getting up fifteen minutes earlier than you normally do, and spending that time working on your top priority, may be difficult at first. But this is how you make BIG progress in your life.

Your morning victories start with preparing properly the night before. You must have a plan in place to take action the next morning. The earlier you rise, the fewer opposing forces to your self-control, and the more momentum you'll have to overcome the inertia of procrastination.

For example, here is my daily routine.

4 a.m. – Writing Session #1

6:30 a.m. – Meditation, Dog Walk, and Breakfast

8 a.m. – Writing Session #2

10:30 a.m. – Early to Rise Team Meeting

11 a.m. – Exercise (four days per week)

12 p.m. – Reading and Lunch

2 p.m. – Phone Calls and Email

4 p.m. – Dog Walk, Big Thinking, and Gratitude Journaling

5 p.m. – Reading, Dinner, and Family/Social Time

8 p.m. – Bedtime

Now, I know what you're thinking. How can I go to bed at 8 p.m.? It's simple. All I've done is shift my schedule ahead a few hours from the norm. When social events keep me up past my preferred bedtime, I do my best to remain true to my wake-up time of 4 a.m. and I make up for lost sleep with an afternoon nap.

Working in these early hours is vital to achieving my big goals and dreams and leaving a legacy in my life. This is what I call Magic Time.

Your Magic Time is where you can get three times as much work done as you would at any other time of the day. We all have our own Magic Time where we are more focused, energetic, and creative. For most people it is first thing in the morning. Your job is to identify your Magic Time, to block it off and ruthlessly protect it from others, and to use it to your advantage. Leveraging this powerful opportunity is essential to making big progress every day.

Let me be clear: You don't have to get up at 4 a.m. You don't even have to get up at 6 a.m. (although it probably wouldn't hurt). The key is to start getting up fifteen minutes earlier than you are normally getting up right now so that you can accomplish something every morning before the chaos of the afternoon sets in.

Research shows that beginning your day with a victory puts you in a positive mood. This morning momentum leads to more victories and continued progress throughout the day.

You also win your health battles early in the morning. Making time to exercise and choosing the right foods for the first meal of the day will help you make better decisions all day long. The right decisions will give you more energy so that you will be more productive, mentally sharp, and free from fatigue—and even pain—all day long.

Your first victory sets the proverbial ball rolling. This first win is also the biggest win and one that no one can take away from you. That's why you must start early and control your morning, so that (barring external emergencies) your day will go exactly as planned.

THREE

THE SECRET TO WINNING YOUR MORNINGS

Warren Buffett is a man of routine. He is early to rise, getting up before 7 a.m. He drinks the same number of Coca-Colas (five) each day, and he prefers to eat a big steak dinner at Gorat's Steak House each night. Most importantly, he avoids meetings and spends 90% of his day reading and thinking. His routine is the foundation upon which he has built a great fortune.

Structure. Rules. Rituals. Organization. Planning. These are keys to success, yet these character traits get a bad rap in today's world. The average person connects discipline and structure with less freedom, not more. Nothing could be further from the truth.

Say you are an investor, like Buffett. Investors know that

patience, discipline, a structured approach, rules for finding specific investments, and an organized plan for investing are all key elements of a successful portfolio. Why then do you not see control of your time in the same way? Why would you think anything but a well-planned day would lead to maximum productivity and progress?

A haphazard approach to investing does not work. We all know that. Well, this goes for investments in both the market and how you use your time each day.

You must harness these feelings of power, control, and ultimately freedom into the internal motivation you need to commit to this daily practice. Nothing comes easy at first but anything important is worth fighting for.

It is tempting to go with the crowd and stay up late each night, watching television or drinking too much alcohol, and sleep late the next morning. That is the way of the average man and gets us nothing but average results in a world where average has now become unacceptable, unbearable, and unrewarding.

Rules, habits, and rituals can help you kick procrastination to the curb and change your life.

Success is simple once you accept how hard it is. It may sound counterintuitive but once you accept how difficult it is going to be, then and only then will you be mentally willing to accept the challenges that it will require, such as sacrifice, dedication, preparation, planning, and perseverance. If you accept these facts, and you must, then it is a simple process of doing the work to create your Perfect Day. You'll simply put your head down and do it.

You must be willing to match your level of desire with the same level of action and commitment to success. Your rules will help you do this. Stop worrying what others think, as Epictetus says, and set yourself on a course of self-mastery. "Once you have determined the spiritual principles you wish to exemplify, abide by these rules as if they were laws," Epictetus said.

Creating your rules for living and sticking to them will guide you to a life of success and wisdom. Though no one will ever be perfect at keeping to the rules, you will be better for trying.

If you drink too much, create a rule that states: "I do not have more than two drinks in one evening." If you eat too much too late at night, create a rule that says: "I do not eat past 7 p.m." If you talk poorly of others, create a rule that declares: "I do not gossip or talk badly about people."

Commit to your rule. Believe in it. Follow the rule as if it were law. Uphold it as if breaking it would put you in jail.

Is this odd? Maybe. Is it extreme? Perhaps. But if you want advanced results you must take advanced measures, even if they seem extreme. What have you got to lose? Where did the average approach to living ever get anyone?

Your rules for living align your actions with your big goals and dreams. Your rules bring you greater accomplishment and success. Your rules will also bring you criticism.

Most people are unwilling to match their dreams with the commitment needed to achieve them. They worry too much about what others think of them. They don't want to sacrifice tonight's TV shows for tomorrow's victories. But having your rules is the secret to winning your mornings. Here's how you will benefit from your rules for living:

- You will have fewer regrets.
- You will no longer wake up vowing to "never do that again."
- You will have a strong framework for success.
- You will have multiple solutions to your obstacles.
- You will have strength against temptations.
- You will have less guilt, fear, frustration, and worry.
- You will experience greater opportunity and attract success and positive people.
- You will reap extraordinary rewards.

Your rules are an essential part of success. Use your rules for living as a clear set of personal philosophies that will make your daily decisions easier. With your rules, you will own your days, achieve your big goals, and leave a lasting legacy. What will yours be?

FOUR

THE ESSENTIAL RULES FOR YOUR LIFE

Imagine you're at a party where the wine is flowing, but the next day you need to get up at 6 a.m. to start a long journey. You've made the decision to avoid alcohol, but the host is persistent. "Are you sure you don't want a drink?" they ask again and again. "We bought a bottle of your favorite wine," they add, testing your willpower, giving you a guilt trip, and introducing stress to what should have been a relaxing evening.

I know how tough it is to say no in situations like this.

Now imagine the same situation but you are three months pregnant. You have a rule that you do not consume alcohol. Period. End of story.

That is the power of having rules in place for your life.

I first recognized the power of rules, or what you can also call

Personal Philosophies, in the Body Transformation Contests that I run in my fitness business, Turbulence Training. The men and women who won these contests and were able to lose fifteen, twenty, or even thirty-five pounds in just twelve weeks all had one thing in common. They all stuck to a set of personal rules that they used to overcome temptation and to stick to their diet and exercise plans.

Here's another example. This time, imagine you're at a backyard cookout. The host is pressuring guests to eat giant cheeseburgers. For you, it's a challenge to say no. You want to stick to your diet, and you're really not that hungry, but the guilt and temptation make you cave.

On the other hand, the person across the table from you is a vegan, and under no circumstances will they ever eat meat. They do not capitulate to peer pressure, thinking, *Well, everyone else is having a cheeseburger, so I will too*. That's not how it works, not when a vegan has a strong personal philosophy that they never, ever, ever eat meat.

Don't dismiss the idea because you think it is too rigid. We all follow rules every day. We stop at red lights. We don't litter. We follow the Ten Commandments. Doing so keeps us out of trouble, stress-free, happy, and productive.

Likewise, your personal rules clearly and concisely outline acceptable behaviors for your life. Your rules state what you will and will not do. Your rules automatically dictate that you make the right decisions, making it easy to overcome obstacles and resist temptation. Your rules replace your reliance on willpower to get you through challenges. Your rules guide you to greater productivity and guilt-free behavior that is congruent with, and supportive of, your goals.

When my clients had rules in place, success was almost inevitable. It made their lives so much easier, and their progress so much more consistent and predictable.

After years of watching my clients transform their lives with rules in place, I finally created my 12 Rules for Living. The purpose of my rules is not to tell you what is right or wrong or to tell you exactly how to live your life. Your rules are your rules. My rules are mine. My rules are simply to serve as an example as you create your own for the sake of living a more productive, stress-free life.

Think of your rules as a way to eliminate your bad habits and replace them with positive routines that make the right decisions almost automatic. You may already have yours outlined in your mind, but I encourage you to put them in writing and to use them to improve every aspect of your life, from family to faith to finances to fitness.

Here are my 12 Rules for Living:

1. I go to bed and get up at the same time seven days per week (8 p.m. and 4 a.m., respectively). I stick to my diet, avoid caffeine after 1 p.m., and avoid alcohol within three hours of bedtime.

2. I write for at least sixty minutes first thing every morning.

3. I do not check email before noon and I do not talk on the phone unless it is a scheduled interview or conference call.

4. I act polite and courteous, and I do not swear.

5. I create a to-do list at the start & end of every workday and update my daily gratitude & achievement journal.

6. I do not engage in confrontations with anyone, in-person or online. This is a waste of time and energy. If I have caused harm, I apologize and fix the situation. And then I take a deep breath, relax, breathe out, and re-focus my efforts back on my work and goals.
    → "Nothing matters." – I can only work towards my big goals and my vision of helping others, while the opinions of others do not matter.
    → "It will all be over soon." – Everything, both good and bad, comes to an end. I must enjoy the good while it lasts, and persevere through the bad until I have beaten it.

7. Everything that happens to me—good and bad—is my personal responsibility. I blame no one but myself. These are the choices I've made—this is the life I'm living. I accept the consequences of my actions.

8. I will help ten million men and women transform their lives.

9. I will not be the person I don't want to be. I will not be petty, jealous, or envious, or give in to any other of those lazy emotions. I will not gossip or speak badly of others,

no matter who I am with or what environment I am in. I will not be negative when it is easier to be positive. I will not hurt others when it is possible to help. I will know the temptations, situations and environments in life that I must avoid, and I will, in fact, avoid them, even if it means loosening relationships with others who "live" in those environments. It's my life and that matters more than what other people think of me.

10. "I will always keep the child within me alive." – Frank McKinney. I will make time to laugh and play every day.

11. "I will write with honesty and feeling." – Ted Nicholas. The opinion of others does not matter. What matters is the number of people that I can help by sharing advice and encouragement in my writing.

My 12 Rules have made me much happier and have eliminated much of the stress in my life.

There will be two types of reactions to the idea of rules. First, some will dismiss it—and dismiss me. The point of the list is not for you to sit there and think, *What a loser. He is so boring.* The reason for sharing my rules is to stimulate the creation of your rules so that you make better decisions in your life.

Every day we get pressured into decisions that leave us full of guilt and remorse. We make better decisions when we have strong personal philosophies in place that guide us.

Wouldn't you be better off if you could make more of the right decisions with less effort?

Of course, and that is where your rules come into play.

You now have a model so that you can create your own rules that will allow you to make fewer decisions that you regret later.

As a result of making more correct decisions and relying less on willpower, you'll move closer to your goals and suffer less frustration. Life will be simpler once you start adhering to your own personal philosophies—and not worrying about what others think.

FIVE

WHAT TO DO ON A PERFECT DAY

Get milk. Pick up the kids. Walk the dog. Wait in line for new iPhone. Such is the curse of the pedestrian to-do list. It inspires nothing, and instead fills in our day with activity but no great accomplishments. The Perfect Day requires better. It needs more.

Despite the technological advances in the world, a simple to-do list remains the secret of successful people. One needs not the latest app or smartphone to best use this powerful tool. What remains a problem, despite centuries of use, is how to properly construct a to-do list that allows you to finish what matters, rather than contributing to your frustration.

The biggest pitfall is biting off more than you can chew, or perhaps said better, writing down more than you can do. As so often happens at a buffet, our eyes are bigger than our appetites, and we take more than we need. Likewise, at the dawn of a new day, we think we are capable of achieving so much more, forgetting that the chaos of the afternoon brings time-thieves that stop us from getting much done.

Having too many activities on your list diffuses your efforts and slows your progress. The result is frustration and unhappiness. You feel like you are getting nowhere. And when you don't move ahead, you grow closer to quitting.

Breaking down your to-do list goals into what are called process goals will help you realistically set your schedule and, more importantly, accomplish what you set out to achieve. Scripting and scheduling tasks, complete with a beginning and end time or goal, will allow you to make the progress you so desperately seek.

Vague goals, such as wanting to lose weight, get rich, or become a writer, can intimidate you out of action. You are better to make specific process goals, such as writing a daily word quota or dedicating a specific amount of time to writing each day. Block time for this process goal in your daily script. Soon the book will be written and you will become a writer, and on a day-to-day basis, you will achieve progress, maintain momentum, and be happier.

The best to-do list sticks to a handful of very specific, actionable, and non-conflicting items. Schedule your number one priority first. Attack it immediately in the morning. Start there and you will win your morning hours and you will own your day.

SIX

CREATING YOUR PERFECT DAY

Imagine you're on holiday in Rome but you forgot to prepare a plan to see the sights. You hop in a cab and get dropped off in front of the Colosseum (the only landmark you know to visit). Then what? Do you wander around? Do you get in another cab and ask for the next tourist trap? If you went about this inefficient way of seeing the Eternal City, would you feel like your time was well spent at the end of the day? Likely not. A wise traveler starts with a plan, even if it's just making sure they have a list of things to see. That's better than nothing.

Most people start their days the same way as the unprepared traveler. The average person lives a reactive life. They get up. They fight to make it to work on time. That's the extent of their planning. They haven't looked any further ahead. They figure that when they get to work, then they'll figure out something to do, or worse, a way to simply get through the day.

They wait to be told what to do or react to whatever emergencies are thrown their way.

A lack of preparation handicaps us in all areas of life. Novice writers sit down in front of a blank screen and hope that inspiration will hit. Newbies to the gym go in, hop on a useless piece of cardio equipment, and go through the motions for twenty minutes with the wishful thinking that somehow this will make up for the 2,000-calorie appetizer they had at Applebee's last night (where they didn't plan ahead to stick to their diet).

Ben Franklin once said, "If you fail to plan, you plan to fail."

You know the power of planning and preparation. You just aren't doing it right for life.

To get more done and have your best days ever, it all begins the night before with creating a to-do list and scripting and scheduling your workdays.

You need a daily schedule. Writers need an outline for writing. If you want to lose weight, you need an exercise program and a meal plan. It's Boy Scouts 101. Always be prepared.

A missing link in your success is Scripting Your Day. Without this act, it's impossible for you to be as effective, efficient, and productive as you can be. Your daily routine gives you a rough template for each day. If we know our priorities, we can build our routine, scripting out tomorrow *today* in order to maximize the time and effort spent working towards what matters.

Your script must start with getting up fifteen minutes early. You can do it. It's not any harder than the transition you made from a late-sleeping college student to getting up at 8 a.m.— or earlier—for your first job after graduation. You survived that lifestyle change, and you will easily survive changing your current schedule to get up fifteen minutes earlier tomorrow. It's not that difficult and the benefits are priceless.

Your script also requires you to set start and end times for all tasks, phone calls, and meetings. This avoids time vampires from sucking your schedule dry.

To create the rest of your script, you must use what I call Reverse Goal Setting. This method of goal setting focuses on working backwards to plan your days. You start at the finish line and run your race in reverse.

For many people, the finish line is about family. You want to be home for dinner. You want to have time with your kids. You want time to talk to your significant other, to read a good book, and to relax in bed. You are tempted to squeeze a million activities—some productive and many insignificant—into your day. That's where things go wrong. That's where the inessential bogs you down and stresses you out. Trying to do too much will ruin a Perfect Day. Reverse goal setting prevents this mistake.

Start by setting a deadline for your workday. If you want to be home by 5:30 p.m. and your commute will take thirty minutes, then that means you must leave the office at 5 p.m. To leave the office at 5 p.m., you'll need to stop working on big tasks at 4:30 p.m. so you can tidy up, prepare for the next morning, go through a simple life-changing end of workday ritual (more about this in a moment), and dash off any last emails or notes to colleagues about important projects or meetings for the next day.

If you start work at 9 a.m., that gives you seven hours of work (depending on the length of your lunch and mid-day breaks).

Even if your career involves a lot of travel, as mine does, we can still follow a general routine to be highly productive on the road. We must get to the airport early, and after we slog through the security rigmarole, we must find a chair, open our laptops, and work as if we were in a more hospitable environment. I've even found that I can meditate as easily on a plane as I can at home. Such are the rituals of the road warrior.

Your script is vital to your success. You must plan your days so that you know what you will get done. You must prepare for your mornings so that you start the day organized, and are able to attack the number one priority in your life first thing in the morning. Your daily script is easy to follow when you build it around your number one priority and you have your NOT-to-do list in place to keep you out of temptation. This structure makes the right behaviors easier to follow.

Scripting your day also allows your subconscious mind to work at night for you while you sleep. When your brain has its to-do list, it will generate ideas while you rest. That's why you often wake up in the middle of the night with ideas. Keep a pen and paper handy at the side of your bed so that you can jot down your big ideas at 2 a.m. or first thing in the morning when you wake up. Those ideas are often like slippery little fish and get away for good if you don't capture them immediately. This is another reason why it is so important to go right to work on your priority tasks if they involve creative work. Dive right into your day without wasting time on preparation or procrastination, or letting your big ideas slip away.

Your least important tasks should be scripted for the time of day when you have the least mental energy. I do not check my email until after I have been working for several hours. This protects my time and energy.

Script your schedule to have a dedicated time, preferably as late in the day as possible, where you deal with email. But until then, stay out of your email inbox as long as you can and control the amount and urgency of email messages in your day. People should not contact you through email if there is an emergency. They should be trained—and yes, trained is the right word for it—to contact you via phone.

If you persist in setting up a system that reduces the number of emails you get each day, you will have less of a need to check email, and therefore it can wait until later and later in the day. With that system in place, it simply becomes a matter of training your email willpower to stay out of your inbox. Day-by-day, minute-by-minute, you can go longer and longer without checking email. It is possible.

I used to be an email addict myself. Back in 2006, just after I transitioned from being a personal trainer to a full-time writer, I immediately rebelled against early mornings and good email hygiene. I slept late, until 7:30 a.m. When I woke up, I immediately opened my email on my Blackberry, wasting the first hour of my day. Worst of all, there was often at least one negative message such as a harsh critique of my work that would throw my day off track.

Of course, I didn't have a well scripted day back then either, and my life was reactive instead of proactive. That was when I began my Perfect Day transformation. After realizing the error of my ways, I began to get up earlier, five minutes at a time. I cancelled my work email account from being forwarded to my phone. Each morning I fought to stay out of my inbox a few minutes longer. It was then that I made a rule—and thus started my Not-to-do list—by making a pledge to not check my email before 9 a.m. It was tough. Many mornings were painful. Some still are. Research shows that checking email delivers the same powerful dopamine response as sugar or drugs. That's why email has a powerful hold on many of us, but it's also why we must work so hard to beat it.

Within a few weeks I had built up the strength to stay out of my email until 9 a.m. Over the months and years it crept to 10:30 a.m., 11 a.m., 12 p.m., and today I check email only three days per week at 2 p.m. for a maximum of two hours. This has opened up my schedule to focus on work that matters. On weekends I'm able to give my full attention to family and friends. On Sundays, I do not use the Internet or my mobile phone at all.

Without email we are better able to concentrate on what

counts, but it's unlikely that you will be able to kick the email hold in a day. You won't wake up tomorrow and be able to go device-free without withdrawal. That's understandable. But you will be able to delay checking your inbox for at least five minutes. Combine that with getting up five minutes earlier tomorrow and that frees up ten minutes of productive time in the morning. It sounds insignificant but it will allow you to accomplish so much. Ten extra minutes in the morning gives you an extra hour of productivity per week, and fifty hours in a year, all without working later at night.

Now you get to celebrate. I highly recommend that, at the end of the day, you use the Early to Rise Gratitude and Achievement Journal. Research shows that our motivation is driven by a sense of accomplishment. Writing down achievements, even if they were small, reminds us that we moved closer to our goals each day. It might be that you made a call to get a project moving. You might have stuck to your goal of writing 1,000 words for your book—as I did and will be grateful for today.

List your accomplishments for the day along with who and what you are grateful for in life. This little exercise takes just five minutes but brings more fulfillment and happiness into your life. It's important to be reminded of all the good things we have in life and the progress we have made. It's what keeps us getting up early, staying out of our inbox, and having our best days ever.

The scripted day is the best day. The best day leads to a great life. A great life ensures a lasting legacy. Each minute is a battle to be won. Make the right decisions with your time. This is the only life you have—and that's why it needs to be planned in great detail.

SEVEN

WHAT NOT TO DO ON A PERFECT DAY

"My nights during my last five years of my drinking always ended with the same ritual: I'd pour any beers left in the refrigerator down the sink," said Stephen King, the author of my favorite book, *The Stand*. "If I didn't, they'd talk to me as I lay in bed until I got up and had another. And another. And one more."

I sincerely hope you don't have the same struggles with alcohol as King. But we all have our Achilles' heel. Perhaps yours is television or junk food. You know you should turn off the television and do some activity, but just as you're about to leave your living room a pizza commercial comes on and you sit back down onto your comfortable couch. You are a little hungry, you think. Maybe you'll just have a quick snack. And then a snooze. Before you know it you've lost all motivation.

Such is life. We are constantly fighting temptations that try to derail our best intentions at every turn. Let's be honest. The obstacles in life far exceed the easy paths to success. Obstacles can knock you off guard. They can destroy all of your hard work, even years of it, in just seconds.

Chocolate, alcohol, pizza, lust, power, greed. They all pull us in the wrong direction.

How do you make the right decisions to overcome the temptations and obstacles in life so that you can succeed at work and at home? What can we do to be more like the transformation champion and less like the weak-willed human that we are?

It starts with your rules and creating your to-do list. But we also need something else. Our temptations are so pervasive; our flaws, so easily exposed. Our weaknesses make us so vulnerable. Humans, it sometimes seems, are built to fail.

The answer is to have a NOT-to-do list.

Having a not-to-do list is a powerful way to support the structure in your day and the freedom you want for your life. There is only so much that you can do, and do well. We must all say NO to things in life. If we didn't, we'd all be working 24 hours a day and it would drive us all to an early grave.

Be clear about what you will and will not do each day. Be clear about what you will not do for success. Some items are easy. You will not lie, cheat, and steal. Those don't necessarily need to be written down. But you need to be clear that you:

- Do not hit the snooze button when you wake-up.
- Do not check email first thing in the morning.
- Do not answer every phone call that comes in at all hours of the day.
- Do not mindlessly surf the Internet.
- Do not waste time gossiping or arguing with colleagues about non-work-related topics.
- Do not consume food or drink that makes you tired or unwell.

You will need to add specific items that identify your individual weaknesses and the obstacles that come your way each day. You must make a list of not-to-do items so that you do not succumb to temptation in the morning when your willpower and discipline are strongest. The morning is the greatest opportunity you will have to make progress. This is where you must win the battle for your day and the war for your future.

Make an honest assessment of what will throw you off track. Identify these interlopers and banish them from your battlefield. The best way to avoid any item on your not-to-do list is to implement rules that make it all but impossible to do the wrong thing. If you have a system, it will make the right actions automatic. That is how you win the morning and have a Perfect Day.

Be strong and build your clear and concise not-to-do list. Add to it when you find an obstacle that is significantly sucking away your time. You will also find it helpful to identify two solutions for each not-to-do obstacle, should you find yourself giving into temptation. This will give your day more structure, and allow you to earn more freedom for your family, friends, and hobbies.

Be thorough with your list and ruthless with your time. You can't do everything. Every wasteful activity in life robs you of moments you could spend focusing on your family, friends, and health. You must draw the line somewhere. Cut out the minutiae, win your morning, control your day, and know what you will NOT do.

If you want to be productive and successful, you can't let your worst behaviors become your habits. Avoiding the wrong things, as Warren Buffett said, is just as important as taking action on your big priorities in life. If you find yourself in a rut, doing the same wrong things over and over again, then you must take on the task of spending time in introspection.

Often it is not heroic actions that bring us success. It is more about simply avoiding temptation and keeping out of trouble. It's what we are able to avoid that allows us to stay on track and achieve superior results. For example, a dieter who can stay away from a Pizza Hut buffet will make greater progress than a jogger who goes to Pizza Hut and rewards themselves with a 2,000-calorie meal after their daily run. An investor who refuses to put money into risky investments won't lose their nest egg. An alcoholic who stays out of bars will have an easier time staying sober.

If you don't want to eat potato chips, don't put them in a bowl within arm's reach or store them in plain sight. Hide them away in your cupboards, or better yet, keep them out of your house. For most people, if it's in the house, we'll eat it. So you must simply keep temptation out of the house just like a recovering alcoholic must stay out of bars. You must ruthlessly eliminate temptations from your day.

You have the systems and strength to overcome the snooze button, to say no to alcohol, to make the right choices at dinner, to protect your mornings and get your work done first thing in the day. You can win your days when you plan ahead—not only for what to do right but also for what to avoid. When you combine a specific plan with a will to win, a never-give-up attitude, and of course action, you will overcome temptations and make the right decisions.

You can navigate your way to success through the landmines that the world has set up in your way. You just need to be prepared. Take five minutes tonight and create that plan. List your weaknesses. Then identify two solutions to beat each one.

Eliminating temptations may require going to extremes as you break the hold of your addictions. Such is the level of effort required to get free of bad habits. Once you do, your rules and newly developed automatic actions will take over to protect you and help you make the right decisions.

You must have rules to address your most offensive behaviors. For the dieter struggling with night eating, you could have a rule that you do not eat after a certain time at night, or that you go twelve hours between dinner and breakfast. For the writer who wants to finish their first book, you could have a rule that you write for ninety minutes first thing in the morning. For the person who wants to break a bad habit, you could create a modified version of my tenth rule ("I will not be the person I don't want to be...") to address your shortcomings.

When you commit to your rules, you'll have greater strength to overcome temptation. Rules are stronger than willpower. Rules are better than habits. Rules are essential to your success.

Deliver yourself from temptation, remove the bad habits from life, replace them with positive rituals and strict rules, and you'll be on track to better days fast.

EIGHT

HOW TO BEAT PROCRASTINATION

It is one of the greatest battles we face each day. We must fight the inertia that slows us down as we fight to take the Hill of Procrastination. The weapons we need in our arsenal are control, focus, persistence, and preparation.

According to an article from *Scientific American*, almost 20% of the population chronically procrastinates, routinely putting off tasks to tomorrow that could be done today. Frankly, that number seems awfully low. Our tendency to procrastinate, first developed pulling all-nighters to cram for exams or finish a term paper, is easily strengthened in today's world of constant social media updates, email addiction, multitasking, and 24-hour news channels. Conquer one vice and another appears.

But for every minute you spend procrastinating, you miss out on a minute of effective study, a minute of making an impact, a minute of moving towards your full potential, or a minute with your family. If procrastination is an issue for you, then let's change that starting right now. Don't wait a minute longer to learn how to tame the beast. Just think of all the amazing accomplishments that you could achieve if you could overcome procrastination.

There are few proven solutions, but they do exist. Beating procrastination takes preparation and knowing your strengths and weaknesses so that you can leverage what works and eliminate what doesn't. But one word of warning: Be careful with your planning techniques and keep them simple. Too often my coaching clients turn planning into its own perverse form of procrastination.

The only thing that helps you overcome procrastination is to be prepared and to actually do the thing you're procrastinating about. That's it. You must take action. You may need to do so robotically. It may be unpleasant, but that's why you're procrastinating, isn't it?

Action is the simplest way to avoid procrastination. Get up and throw yourself into the battle. Be clear about your number one priority and attack it with great energy.

In order to get something done, you must first get started. In order to complete the project, you must do everything that needs to get done. It's not rocket science. It's persistence.

Don't let information gathering become your procrastination.

Don't let planning become your procrastination.

In the end, the decision to move to action comes from behavioral congruence. This means that you act in accordance with what you want to accomplish.

For example, if you say that you want to be on time for work every day, but you stay up past an appropriate bedtime and you don't plan your morning routine, and you hit the snooze button five times, none of that is acting in behavioral congruence with your goals.

Compare what you say you want against what you actually do. Do they match? If not, it's time to change and figure out what really matters. Once you do, line up your priority with the actions you need to achieve it, and then embrace the pain, pay the price, and earn the prize.

You must become the person you need to become in order to achieve the big goals and dreams that you want to achieve. You must do the right planning, take the right actions, make the right decisions, and eliminate the wrong obstacles that tempt you into wrong behaviors. You must arm yourself with the artillery you need to take the Hill of Procrastination.

You can solve this problem by creating your rules that will guide your decisions and actions. Get started there, and then continuously work to improve your behavioral congruence in all aspects of your life.

It is from this structure that you will have more freedom in your life. It sounds paradoxical, but I assure you, the better the rules you have for your life, the more freedom you will enjoy.

NINE

SEVEN STEPS TO BUILD HABITS OF STEEL

When I was in my twenties I was addicted to visiting sports and news websites. Fortunately I recognized the problem and over time developed a simple, quick, and easy solution to snap out of it and get back to work.

You might suffer from the same type of obsessive-compulsive behavior (OCB) such as checking email, visiting news websites, reading text messages, and then returning to your inbox to start all over again. That's how so many of us procrastinate the day away.

Habits, both good and bad, are hard to change. Habits are behaviors deeply ingrained in your nervous system, part of the electrical network connecting your mind with the rest of your body. Every time you default to a bad habit, like visiting a forbidden website or biting your nails, you make the wiring stronger and the habit harder to break.

When we follow our good habits, like getting up early, we strengthen the rituals that win our mornings and bring us Perfect Days.

"Only when habits of order are formed can we advance to really interesting fields of action," wrote the philosopher William James. Habits are the secret to getting ahead in life and achieving your big goals and dreams.

So how do we break those bad habits and overcome OCB? The solution is in having a trigger that reminds you to get back on track. Triggers are little tricks that interrupt your bad habits. For example, turning off your phone or disconnecting from the Internet stops you from repeatedly checking your email or text messages. Brushing your teeth can get you back on track and help you avoid mindless eating at night. Turning on loud, energetic music can be the trigger you need to finally start the exercise session you've been delaying all morning. Pulling out your checkbook and putting on a collared shirt could be the trigger you need to finally sit down and deal with your monthly bills.

These little triggers can go a long way.

I developed a trigger to deal with my Internet addiction. If I caught myself in my bad habit, I just had to summon up the smallest amount of discipline to open up the Microsoft Word program on my computer. That was the trigger that snapped me out of my procrastination. It triggered a break in my bad habit and a return to the right actions.

I still use this trick today when I am tempted by trouble. It's the trigger I need to return to my writing. From there, each word typed was a victory. Each sentence a battle won. Each paragraph was a huge step in conquering the procrastination demon. Every victory makes it easier to achieve the next. I get on a roll and then it's hard to stop working and easy to avoid procrastination.

That's the big lesson. Action begets action. And it all starts with a simple trigger.

Identify a trigger to get you into action mode and out of temptation. It doesn't need to be anything fancy. It doesn't need to cost money or require another person to help you. It just needs to be an easy yet effective reminder that triggers you to get back to the task at hand.

Now if you're ready to build on that and create Habits of Steel, here's what you need to do:

Step #1 – Figure Out What Matters…and Focus On It

What's more important to your legacy, checking CNN headline news and ESPN sports scores or writing your first book, securing your dream job, and providing for your family? The answer is obvious. Success requires us to do the first things first. Choose to use your time wisely. Figure out what really matters to you and then use the rest of the steps to build habits that allow you to focus your time on it.

Step #2 – Identify Steps to Success and Rules for Your Life

No one will ever be perfect at keeping to their rules, but you will be better for trying, and you will have stronger habits that allow you to avoid the disappointment, guilt, and regret of wasted days.

Step #3 – Create a Checklist for New Habits

Two years ago I began meditating at sunrise. Connecting a positive action, like meditation, with a daily trigger, such as the sunrise, is a great way to create new habits.

Each habit needs to be broken down into action items for you to get started. Take for example my meditation checklist:

- Time the habit with sunrise.
- Start with a quick brain dump of ideas to clear my head.
- Set a pillow on the floor to sit upon for proper positioning.
- Turn off the lights in the room (slowly make way to pillow without stubbing toes!).
- Sit on the pillow, cross-legged, and breathe slowly and deeply from my belly.
- Focus on my breathing to help clear my mind.
- Continue until I feel a sense of calm come over me.

Step #4 – Prepare the Night Before

Winning habits begin with proper planning. Prepare your

checklist. Lay out an easy-to-follow pathway for success. Set out any tools you will need to do the first things first.

Step #5 – Remove All Obstacles

Removing obstacles, temptations, and bad habits is one of the most important changes you can make in life. Eliminating the negatives is often more important for success than relying on willpower for the creation of new habits. When you remove temptations from your day, it becomes much easier to make and stick to the right decisions.

No matter what your number one priority in the morning, whether it is writing, Bible study, or exercise, make sure that you are prepared so that nothing else gets in your way. You must remove temptations that allow procrastination. For example, make sure your Bible is opened to the correct page and place it on your desk, so you see it there rather than your phone or computer. Or lay out your exercise clothes so that you don't have to search through your drawers to find them.

Step #6 – Take Massive Action

We can control what time we wake up, what habits we start the day with, what temptations enter—and are eliminated— from our lives, and what systems we have in place for dealing with all of these. We can believe in ourselves or we can have doubt. It's our choice.

"To live a life of virtue, match up your thoughts, words, and deeds," said Epictetus. Practice what you preach, take action on what you teach. Oh, and a little incentive never hurts. Give yourself a prize for taking action and following through. We repeat what we reward. It can be as simple as enjoying the beauty of a sunrise as you meditate. Find what you need to trigger your new habit.

Step #7 – Learn & Improve

Few days will be easy. Most days will require you to fight tooth-and-nail to stick to your habits and achieve your goals. On those days, take the opportunity to learn from your mistakes and struggles. They will make you stronger.

That's the power of routine, the importance of habit. Each day that we make the right decisions and take the right actions will make it a little easier to repeat in the future. When you follow these seven steps, you'll find a way to build the right habits in all areas of your life.

TEN

THE 10-3-2-1-0 GOODNIGHT FORMULA TO GUARANTEE FIFTEEN MINUTES OF FREEDOM

The single most important factor in winning your mornings and owning your days is to get up fifteen minutes earlier and work on your number one priority before anyone else is awake. It's that simple. In theory, that is. But with all the chaos and temptations in life, how do you do it? Well, it's easy to be well rested and get up on time when you use this 10-3-2-1-0 formula.

This system helps you get to bed on time, sleep better, and wake up the next morning well rested and ready for battle.

10 hours before bed – No more caffeine.

3 hours before bed – No more food or alcohol.

2 hours before bed – No more work.

1 hour before bed – No more screen time (turn off all phones, TVs and computers).

0 – The number of times you will hit the snooze button in the morning.

Stop drinking all caffeinated beverages ten hours before bed. This is generally the amount of time required for your body to clear it from the bloodstream and eliminate its stimulatory effects.

Finish eating big meals and drinking alcohol three hours before bed. This will help you avoid heartburn (gastric reflux) and interrupted sleep. Alcohol might make you feel sleepy, but it impairs your natural sleep cycle and interrupts valuable deep sleep.

End all work-related activities two hours before bed. No more taking phone calls, checking emails, reading reports, or thinking about tomorrow.

If you struggle to find the "off button" for your brain, I can relate. But at the end of your day, in order to enjoy uninterrupted time with family, in order to be present for your children, in order to forget about work problems, tasks that didn't get done, or items that need to get completed first thing in the morning, you need to do a Brain Dump. It's a simple solution that takes five minutes and requires nothing more than a blank piece of paper and a pen.

Here's what you'll do. Write down everything going through your head. Write fast and furious. Get it all out. Now take that paper and set it aside, perhaps in your office or at the front door under your car keys. Now forget about it for the rest of the day. It can wait until tomorrow. That will help clear your mind. Do that brain dump, plan out your morning, and leave it behind so that you can wind down with family time and getting ready for bed.

Turn off all electronics one hour before bed. The blue light emitted from screens makes it difficult to fall asleep. Spend the final hour reading real books, talking with your spouse, meditating, taking a bath, or enjoying "other" activities in the privacy of your bedroom—but do not use your iPhone or tablet, unless you want to stare at the ceiling for another hour.

The last temptation to avoid comes first thing in the morning. If you wake up to the sound of an alarm, you will be tempted to hit the snooze button. Don't. Not only will it make you late for your scripted day and interfere with winning your morning, but going back to sleep for a few minutes actually makes you more tired than if you had started your day immediately.

There are solutions to help you overcome the temptation of the snooze button. First, place your alarm across the room. That makes you get up, leave your bed, and walk a few steps before you can turn it off. By then, you're more awake and it's easier to resist the allure of snoozing. Of course, that approach could also result in divorce, or at least being told to sleep on the couch.

A second, more stoic approach is to internalize the benefits of getting up immediately. Remember why you are doing this. It's your one and only life, one that is not rewarded for staying in bed, one that does not move forward because you stole an extra five minutes of sleep. If you want more sleep, you need to get to bed earlier, not wake up later. You cannot miss out on your magical fifteen minutes in the morning. Don't let your opportunity slip away. You've already invested effort into the 10-3-2-1 portion of the formula. Don't let it all go to waste now. You can do it. You've done it before, perhaps on days when you've had to get up and get to the airport on time for an early flight, and you can do it tomorrow morning, too. No excuses. Controlling your morning and winning your days starts at minute zero. Don't lose the momentum in your life to the snooze button. Start winning your day immediately.

ELEVEN

PUT THE BIG THREE INTO PLACE

Whether you are building a business, raising a family, training for a triathlon, writing a newsletter, managing people, or selling real estate, your morning rituals and routines establish your success. Here's the plan you must have in place:

- Get up fifteen minutes earlier starting tomorrow.
- Know your number one priority and go to work on it immediately.
- Use your rules to create rituals and routines to overcome obstacles, eliminate temptation, and end procrastination in your life.
- Replace bad habits with new good ones.
- Get to bed on time.

Out of those steps, the one that gives you the most leverage and bang-for-your-buck is to create rules. Don't be intimidated by my list. Start small. Here are the three most important rules you need to create for your life:

1. State what time you go to bed and get up every day.

2. Write down the number one action step you will take each morning that moves you closer to your big goals and dreams. It could be work, it could be writing, it could be exercise. Choose the right priority activity for you.

3. Create a Simple Health Plan. Do you need to meditate, exercise, eat better, or sleep more? In your health rule, state what you don't eat (so that you find it easier to avoid food temptations), when you go to bed, when you meditate or pray, or when and how you exercise.

Identify the habits that you need to have in place to support your rules. Those are the solutions that will help you stick to your rules and you should add these to your daily schedule.

Once you have those in place and have spent a few weeks perfecting your morning system, take your rules to the next level. Create rules for how you will control your schedule, how you will deal with emails, phone calls, and meetings, how you will limit vices and temptations, and how you will deal with others and the stress they bring to your life.

With these rules, habits, and schedules in place, the morning is yours, the day is won, and you will control your life, no matter how much chaos is thrown at you. You'll discover how to deal with that next.

PART II

CONQUER THE AFTERNOON

TWELVE

MAKE IT PERSONAL

In 2008, my future client Catherine Gordon suffered a humiliating experience at her local grocery store. At the checkout counter, the clerk offered her the senior's discount. She was only forty-five. Hiding the tears in her eyes, she vowed that day to transform her life. Just a few weeks later, after losing fourteen pounds, she looked fourteen years younger and won the grand prize in my Turbulence Training Fat Loss Transformation Contest.

After reading Catherine's winning entry, I discovered that she had put five principles into play that guaranteed success. As time went on, I found that every winner of the Transformation Contest used these same rules. I call them the 5 Pillars of Success. These are planning & preparation, professional accountability, social support, an incentive, and the big deadline.

If you have all 5 Pillars then you have the foundation to guarantee that you will achieve your number one priority in life, whether it is to lose weight, make more money, or find the person of your dreams. But if one—or more—is missing, then your odds of success decrease dramatically. In this section I'll show you exactly how to add the 5 Pillars to your Perfect Day for rapid results.

Catherine knew one other thing. Success started—and ended—with her Personal Responsibility.

There is an old saying: "If it is to be, it's up to me." That is the cold, hard truth. You, and you alone, are responsible for exactly where you are in life. You are responsible for your friends, your family, your wealth, your health, your energy, your motivation, your days, your nights, your rules, your vision, and your behavior.

When we take personal responsibility for who, what, and where we are in life, it changes our perspective on success. We can now take control of our lives. *"Everything that happens to us—good and bad—is our personal responsibility. We can blame no one else. These are the choices we've made—this is the life we're living. We will accept the consequences of our actions."* This is my eighth Rule for Living, and one that I recommend you adopt in some way.

As time passes, most people will allow themselves to remain in the same place, advancing neither miles nor even inches. Not you. You are in it to win it. You will not take the easy way out and rest on your past victories. The enemy cares not for what you did yesterday. It starts fresh again today. So must you. You know what to do. I don't need to lecture you anymore about the power of preparation. Now it's merely about fine-tuning your mind and creating powerful habits for success.

This is your one-and-only earthly life. You must do what is right for you. Control your mornings, conquer the chaos that others bring into your life, and concentrate on what counts at night.

Your life is your personal responsibility. Use these 5 Pillars to put in place the foundation to support it.

THIRTEEN

THE 1ST PILLAR: PLANNING AND PREPARATION

It was in Anthony Bourdain's book *Kitchen Confidential* that I was first introduced to the concept of *mise-en-place*, an essential ritual for the professional chef. "Meez," as chefs pronounce it, translates into "everything in its place." It requires planning and preparing a place for every tool and ingredient you'll need for cooking a meal. It is the single most important step in creating a great meal, and saves the chef great time and energy. This level of planning and preparation is the key to success for any goal in life.

You must have a physical and mental version of mise-en-place in your life to control your working environment. Take full responsibility for your work environment and behaviors. Everything you do either sets you up for success or puts another obstacle in your way. You must be prepared with the right tools and rituals to make the right decisions for your day. You must eliminate the temptations that stand in your way.

One of the reasons you must attack your number one priority first thing in the morning is that you are armed at that early hour with the greatest willpower to act and avoid getting into trouble. The morning holds the fewest external distractions and temptations from other people. Once you can pry yourself away from bed then you will be able to get to work on your priority without anyone else bothering you. You must get those fifteen magical minutes before anyone else gets up.

Likewise, with proper preparation you can conquer the chaos of the afternoon. If you are a manager, then meeting with others will probably be your number one priority. You can win these meetings in advance with planning. Sit down, go through the meeting agenda, identify the obstacles, build two solutions for each, and be prepared so that the meeting runs on time and achieves the objective. This will help you overcome the obstacles associated with most meetings and you'll win your day and stay on track.

Control requires the removal of temptation, and temptations are individual. Your temptation could be the siren's call of going back to bed. It could be getting sucked into the office drama found within your email inbox. It could be getting obsessed with the negative news of the day. But all of these can wait. You can have a nap later. The office drama will resolve itself. Your email can wait. And there's nothing you can do about something that happened half a world away.

These trivial matters can wait—and MUST wait—until you have made progress on your priority.

Identify your temptations. Write them down. And then plan and prepare to methodically remove them from your morning. If the television tempts you, then do your work in a room without one. If you constantly search the fridge—in procrastination rather than hunger—then work in your basement or attic, far removed from the kitchen. If you struggle not to visit your favorite websites, use a computer that is not connected to the Internet or use a software program that restricts you from the Internet. Do whatever you must do to eliminate distractions and temptations.

Removing temptations is one of the most important actions you can take to keep yourself on track. For example, take a look at how simple actions can eliminate temptations for struggling dieters and then identify ways you can remove your temptations in life.

Nutrition researchers from Cornell University have found that if you place a bowl of candy within arm's reach, then you will eat more of it. That's not surprising. Move the bowl off your desk and you'll eat less. Put the candy in an opaque jar and you will notice it less and consume less of it. Move the jar into another room or hide it in the back of a cupboard that requires a ladder to reach and you'll eat even less. Avoid having candy in the house in the first place and voilà, no temptation at all.

That's the same mindset and approach you must make with all of the temptations that get between you and your work.

It's your job to blow them all up. Some you can conquer with planning and preparation. Some will require elimination. Take stock at the end of a workday and identify the temptations that took you off track. Then destroy them, one by one.

There are many things we want to accomplish in life, but there can be only one number one priority at a time. Know it, attack it, and focus on it every day. Create the right working environment, right now, and conquer your day so you can concentrate on what counts at night.

FOURTEEN

THE 2ND PILLAR: PROFESSIONAL ACCOUNTABILITY, OR THE POWER OF A PRO

The smartest business decision I've ever made was to hire my first business coach. But taking so long to do it was also the biggest mistake I've ever made. Had I not been so cheap and stubborn and procrastinated on getting the professional coaching and accountability that I needed, the impact of my business on the world today would be much bigger.

We all need a coach. Wayne Gretzky, Derek Jeter, Serena Williams, Tiger Woods, and every athlete at the pinnacle of performance always had a coach. We all benefit from having a mentor. Mark Zuckerberg has one. Warren Buffett has one. Steve Jobs had one.

A coach not only teaches us what to do, but holds us accountable for doing it. And that might be the most important role of all. You need professional accountability. You need to be constantly checking in with someone who can give you expert feedback and guide you to making better choices, building better habits, and getting better results.

Research supports this. A study from Stanford University found that being accountable to a professional (such as a doctor, nutritionist, or trainer) was significantly more effective for weight loss than being accountable to a non-expert. For my fat loss Transformation Contest winners, they had me as their professional accountability.

This holds true for all areas you want to improve in life. If you want to make more money, you need a professional manager, mentor, or business coach. If you want to find the love of your life, you'll do better with a relationship coach or professional matchmaker. If you want to eat better, you need a nutrition guru. You can't succeed without proper coaching, let alone trying to do it all on your own.

It also works both ways. When you become a mentor, you will become better. If you are in a position to help others, you must do it, for their benefit and for yours.

Back in my days as a personal trainer to Toronto's elite, my favorite clients were the ones who demanded to know why I was giving them a specific exercise, using a new technique, or encouraging them to eat a certain way.

If I struggled to explain a technique, their critical gazes let me know loud and clear that my reasoning wasn't sound. This caused me to study and hone my craft so that I delivered an even better and more effective workout the next time. Each day I got better and developed more valuable skills. It also helped me improve my own body transformation results.

That's why, if your goal is to transform your life in any way, it's helpful to become a mentor to someone else who seeks the same goals. By explaining your new habits, you will better understand their importance, and furthermore, you will become more committed to these new behaviors. As a teacher you want to maintain integrity and act in a way that is consistent with what you just taught. After all, a hypocrite is a lousy mentor.

"While we teach, we learn," said the Roman philosopher Seneca. From ancient history through today, humans have realized that when you teach others, you end up learning more than the student. That's why the best way to develop a greater understanding of any material is to play the role of the teacher and explain it to a student.

It's even better when your students challenge you. The more questions they ask, and the greater their skepticism, the more you have to dig deep to properly articulate your answers and justify your beliefs. It's much better to teach minds that are actively engaged rather than passive.

Nothing is better than working one-on-one with a cynical

student. It demands that you become a better teacher, and develop a better understanding of the material.

But teaching goes beyond just strengthening your knowledge. Teaching makes you a better person, too.

"You cannot brighten another's path without lighting your own," said my friend and mentor, Frank McKinney.

I believe it. I've experienced it time and time again. There's not much work in the world that can make you feel as fulfilled as teaching others. Each time I step on stage to teach, I forget my selfish worries and problems, and leave the stage a better man. Each time I create a fitness video, it elevates my mood and leaves me satisfied knowing that I've delivered to the world.

This approach is simple to apply in our own lives. Follow these two rules for becoming a wiser and better person: First, you must practice what you preach. Second, you must practice preaching it.

Try it today. Teach someone something. It could be showing your child how to tie their shoes, or it could be sharing a simple productivity tip with a colleague. No matter what you teach, you'll feel better for it.

The big lesson is that if you want to improve yourself, then you MUST become a teacher and mentor to more people.

The teacher always learns as much as, if not more than, the student.

The more you learn, the more you can help others, and the virtuous cycle continues, making you better and better at what you do, and allowing you to help more and more people.

Teaching others can also lift you out of the tough times we all experience in life. When you're down, your best solution is to become the helping hand to someone else.

When you teach others what you know, when you share your knowledge, when you add value, this can help you in so many ways. It can deliver you from (mild) depression and anxiety, from a scarcity mindset, and from a lack of clarity. Teaching will give you a natural high. You'll do something good for others, and better yet, you'll do something great for yourself. All the while you'll improve your understanding of the material.

Every time I've shared my expertise with others, I've left with new ideas, a better understanding, a clearer vision of the problem (and the solution that can be implemented), a feeling of gratitude for the knowledge that I have, and thankfulness for the ability to shine a little light into someone's life.

Don't tell me you don't have anything to teach the world. In most areas of life, you don't need to be a certified instructor or a genius in order to impart a little wisdom to a friend, a colleague, or a mentee. You just need to pass along what you know. Everyone wins when you become a mentor.

Very likely, there's an area in life where you know more than 99% of the world. It's true for almost every person. We all have our distinct strengths. You could share a tip or two each day with colleagues who struggle in any one of those areas. Not only would it boost their performance, but you'd also improve your own work habits. You would also benefit because it would make you more aware and committed to making similar changes in your own life. And of course, it will leave you with a smile on your face when you see the light bulbs go off in their eyes.

"Show your character and commitment through your actions," Epictetus said. It doesn't matter if you are teaching a physical skill or a mental attribute, you cannot be a good teacher without making yourself better. When you instruct by example, it leads you to live by example. The lessons become more deeply ingrained in your mind. And that will make all the difference in your life.

FIFTEEN

THE 3RD PILLAR: SOCIAL SUPPORT, OR HOW TO HARNESS THE POWER OF OTHER PEOPLE

I'm "up" with people. I know there are positive, supportive people out there who want to help you achieve your goals. You must believe this as well. The positive power of other people must be harnessed in your drive to having your best days ever.

For personal and professional goals, this means recruiting a social support network filled with friends and family, employees, business partners, personal assistants, and mentors (both virtual—through books, videos, and online programs—and in-person coaches). Regardless of who is on your list, positive people are a necessity and a reality. Seek them out. Do not stop until you find them. You must recruit staunch allies to support your daily battles, to help you win the war for your mornings, and to heal and recover from your battles.

"Be careful whom you associate with," Epictetus warned. "It is human to imitate the habits of those with whom we interact. We inadvertently adopt their interests, their opinions, their values, and their habit of interpreting events. Though many people mean well, they can just the same have a deleterious influence on you because they are undisciplined about what is worthy and what isn't."

Find people, online and offline, trying to improve the same way you are. Learn from them. Support them in return. Pretend that they are with you at all times, when you want to sleep in, when you want to cheat, when you want to give up, and hear their encouraging words, and take action on their advice. Push on and stay strong, they will say, and that's what you will do. Make the right decisions, right now, with their support. You can always harness the power of positive people, even when they are not around.

This may seem difficult at first. You might have a hard time believing there are any positive people willing to support their dreams. The average person tends to live a "crab in a bucket" existence. If you're not familiar with this mistake of the mind, let me explain.

The story goes like this. Imagine you're visiting Alaska and find yourself walking down a pier. Sitting over the edge of the dock are several local fisherman. Beside each is a bucket. You take a peek inside one of the buckets and notice there are a bunch of small crabs. One is clamoring for the top of the bucket. It looks like there is going to be an escape.

"Hey, mister," you say, "one of your crabs is trying to make a break for it. Better put a lid on that bucket."

The old fisherman chuckles and says to you, "Ha, you must be new around here. Watch this. He ain't going anywhere."

You turn to the bucket. There it is, plain as day. One of the crabs is making an escape like Andy Dufresne from *The Shawshank Redemption*. It has almost climbed to the top of the bucket. *Free at last,* you think. Suddenly, one of the other crabs hauls the potential escapee back down to the bottom of the bucket.

The old fisherman laughs again. "You see, ain't none of those other crabs ever going to let one of the other ones escape," he says. "Them crabs is always safe in the bucket."

That's a far too accurate analogy for the average person's attitude in life. When people see a friend starting to do well and escape their current comfort zone, often bitterness, fear, and jealousy will drive the average person to pull the escapee back down. It might be done through subconscious sabotage. The saboteur might not realize they are being negative and holding you down. Then again, they might be doing everything they possibly can, on purpose, to interfere with your success in life.

That's what we must deal with if we don't make the effort to surround ourselves with positive people. Only with social support can we achieve the escape velocity necessary to leave our Comfort Zone.

"You either become like your companions," Epictetus said, "or you bring them over to your own ways. Great is the danger, so be circumspect on entering into personal associations, even and especially light-hearted ones. We often end up being carried along by the crowd. Choose your associations with care."

Surround yourself with people who inspire you, who make you better, who you respect, and who you look up to. You'll be better for it.

There really are great people out there who want to help you. But many of them are hiding. They hold back their positivity and their goals and dreams because they too have had those dreams crushed by others. Better to keep their desires secret than be ridiculed by friends, family, and co-workers, they think.

How does one escape this? It starts with small steps, making little bets, and doing minor tests. You must proceed cautiously at first. You leak out a small amount of your dreams to someone. You watch their response. If it is supportive, you share a little more. If they laugh at you, tell you it will never happen, or list all of the ways that you're going to fail, then you simply reverse course and strike that person off your list of people that you should be spending time with. You don't have to ban them from your life forever, but be prepared to interact with them on only a superficial level. They are not worthy of your goals, dreams, and aspirations. They are a crab. They'll never leave the bucket, and you won't either if you let them influence your life.

If your friends, family, and co-workers want you to be lazy, fat, unhappy, unproductive, and average, it must stop. You have no other option but to cut back on the time you spend with these people. The time has come for you to stand up for yourself and do what is right for you in the long run. You only have one shot at leaving a legacy for your life. How you use your time and who you spend your time with are the most important decisions you'll make in life. Choose wisely.

You cannot succeed if you let the crabs in the bucket pull you back down. You cannot soar with eagles if all you do is hang around turkeys.

"How long can you afford to put off who you really want to be?" Epictetus asked. "Your nobler self cannot wait any longer. Put your principles into practice—NOW. Stop the excuses and procrastination. This is your life! From this instant on, vow to stop disappointing yourself. Decide to be extraordinary and do what you need to do—now."

Ask the big question: What do you really want to achieve in life? Then think, *are the people I'm spending time with helping me achieve this?*

"The key is to keep company only with people who uplift you, whose presence calls forth your best," Epictetus said. Become the person you need to be to achieve what you want to achieve.

It might seem difficult, but it is essential that you remove negative, stressful, and poisonous attitudes from your life. Cut the cord quickly. Search out more positive people and experiences. Start with books or videos from your local library. Begin to change with the help of virtual mentors. Then build your network. Go online and find new friends through forums and meet-up groups. Begin attending live events in your chosen industry, occupation, or hobby, so that you spend time with people who have the same interest in achievement as you.

The top level of social support in business is found in a Mastermind group. These consist of positive, like-minded, goal-oriented people just like you, and these are led via mentors who have had great success in the past and now want to coach you on your journey. Finding the right social support for your goals is one of the most important steps you can take on the path to success.

SIXTEEN

THE 4TH PILLAR: AN INCENTIVE, OR TREAT YOURSELF TO BIG VICTORIES

As a child, I spent every Sunday morning at First St. John's Lutheran Church. Each week, I would go through the same routine. It started with a bath, followed by my mom painfully combing the "tangles" out of my naturally curly hair. She'd then dress me in my Sunday best, and my uncle would pick me up at 9 a.m. sharp for Sunday School held in the church basement.

At 11 a.m., my sister and I would head upstairs and join my mother in the third pew from the back on the left-hand side. That's where we sat every Sunday morning for over two decades. As I grew older, I developed the discipline to sit through the hour-long service without misbehaving. However, as a six-year old boy anxious to get home to his baseball bats and hockey sticks, sitting still for sixty minutes (and seventy-five minutes during monthly communion service) was a difficult task.

My mother's solution was candy. After about twenty minutes of the service, when boredom began to set in for me and my sister, she brought out rolls of SweeTarts for each of us.

This is where I learned a valuable habit that has helped me succeed in life. I made it my mission every Sunday morning to hold out longer than my sister before eating the candy.

Some weeks I'd hide my candy, pretending I'd eaten it, and then, when I knew my sister was done with hers, I'd produce my treats from my pocket and take great pleasure in eating the tiny candy pieces. On other occasions, it would be a straight-up battle of wills as we both played with our candy in an attempt to see who could hold out the longest.

What I discovered on those Sunday mornings was the power of delayed gratification. As a young boy, I used this skill to "win" at the candy game with my sister. As a teenager, I put this power to use by forcing myself to go to my after-school job, then to the gym to lift weights, and then home to do homework, all before going out with my friends.

In my college years—excluding my freshman year where I let the habit slide—I used delayed gratification to put schoolwork first over late-night partying. I still remember the late Friday nights spent in the lab finishing up my research before finally rushing out to meet my friends at a house party. Using this secret, I earned a spot on the Dean's Honor List three years in a row and won a scholarship that paid for graduate school.

The power of delayed gratification is, in fact, a research-proven phenomenon. There's a famous study that was performed at Stanford University, known as the Stanford Marshmallow Experiment.

Researchers in the 1960s tracked a group of children roughly between the ages of four and six, each of whom was given a marshmallow or other sweet and instructed that, if they waited several minutes before eating it, they could enjoy one additional treat. Researchers continued following this same group of children for five decades to monitor their developmental progress. The study scientists, led by psychologist Walter Mischel, discovered that the children who were better able to wait to eat the marshmallow—delaying gratification— were generally more dependable and had better life success.

Substitute a church pew for a Stanford University research lab and SweeTARTS for marshmallows, and you can see the personal connection I have with this research.

The ability to delay gratification is not something that you must be born with, but it's a powerful habit you can build. Of course, it's not easy. We want it all. And we want it now. We are tempted to spend our paychecks as soon as we get them— or even before. As a result, we sacrifice future success for immediate pleasure. But that's not how it works if you want to be successful. Work comes first. Then reward. It's not the other way around.

No matter where you've stood in the past on this success equation, you can change. We can all learn to get up earlier, make exercise a daily habit, and improve our diet through the habit of delayed gratification.

Like starting a new exercise program, it's going to be hard at first, but you will come to appreciate your new power of habit. The benefits are well worth it. You must look at the work and the struggles as blessings. Practice (i.e. training) is the only way you can build up your delayed gratification muscle and earn the rewards.

Mastery takes time. But mastery is worth the effort.

Take action. Struggle. Fight. Flex. And work.

Keep your eye on the prize. You can do it.

SEVENTEEN

THE 5TH PILLAR: THE BIG DEADLINE, OR THE MOST IMPORTANT PILLAR OF THEM ALL

A few days after Christmas one year, I had to rush my mom to the hospital. She had been having chest pain for days and things were getting worse. Luckily, it turned out to be nothing more than a pulled muscle. But it shook me up. As I waited in the ER, I thought about all of the things—both personal and professional—I wanted to achieve while my mom was still around to see them.

Although it's a terrible thing to think about, I couldn't get the nagging "what if" out of my head all week. We all have a natural Big Deadline in our lives, and the realization that we are all running out of time should be enough to inspire us to take action on our top priority today.

You must learn to harness the power of the Big Deadlines in your life. You've done it before. Think back to the last time you went on vacation. You sure were productive on that final day of work before it started, weren't you? A deadline gets us to take action. It signifies the light at the end of the tunnel, the finish line at the end of the home stretch, that motivates us to accelerate our progress and push harder towards our goals. The deadline puts urgency into our actions and keeps us going through the tough times and dark days. It is what keeps my fat loss clients on track after weeks of avoiding temptation, and it holds the same power for you.

The Big Deadline is the fifth, final, and most important Pillar of Success. Without it, we procrastinate. We put off our best intentions until tomorrow when we should be doing them today. But if you want to succeed, you must have deadlines on your schedule for what really matters in life. They are harsh, honest, and unforgiving. They work like nothing else.

There are two ways the power of the Big Deadline can help you have a Perfect Day.

First, you can use them in your daily routines by setting limits on your workday. For example, Sheryl Sandberg, the COO at Facebook, is famous for setting a rule that she would be home every night at 5:30 p.m. to have dinner with her children. That was a non-negotiable deadline.

Deadlines must also be applied to your daily tasks. It's one thing to plan out a busy day of activities on your to-do list, but if you don't include a cut-off time for them, such as limiting a phone call to no more than twenty minutes, then these activities will all last longer than planned and cut into the amount of work you can accomplish. A jam-packed to-do list with no deadlines can you leave you frustrated due to a lack of progress on what really matters in your life.

The second and more important way to harness the power of the Big Deadline is by setting an end date for achieving your goals. Your dreams must have a deadline. Personal transformation programs work best when set for ninety days or less.

If you want to aggressively pursue success, take your deadline and cut it in half. At first this new deadline might seem near impossible to hit, but after reflection, you should think that yes, you can do it, if you put the 5 Pillars in place for your success.

Challenge yourself. Otherwise you might suffer from Parkinson's law, which says, "Work expands so as to fill the time available for its completion." If you don't have a cut-off date for your projects, then you'll continue to add to your to-do list and the work will drag on forever. If you have a project that is lingering, set a deadline—one that comes with meaningful consequences for missing it—and get it done. Every deadline should come with incentives. You might choose to inflict a punishment upon yourself (such as making a donation to a political party or cause that you dislike) or you might offer yourself a reward for success.

I struggled with Parkinson's law and procrastination when creating my Turbulence Training Fat Loss Certification for personal trainers. My preparation work dragged on and on until I finally set a Big Deadline, booked a filming date, and pre-paid for a conference room and videographer. By setting the filming date with meaningful consequences (paying all that money with nothing to show for it if I weren't ready), the deadline gave me the urgency I needed to get the work done and avoid the punishment of wasting the money spent on the room and film crew.

Deadlines force you to focus and take the actions you need to take in order to achieve your big goals and dreams. There is nothing as powerful as the urgency of a deadline—set with meaningful consequences—to finally get you to take action.

CHAPTER EIGHTEEN: HOW TO USE THE 5 PILLARS IN REAL LIFE

Think back to a time where you had to sit through a boring, wasteful meeting. Maybe you've had one already today.

Recently a friend told me about a nightmare meeting he had. He was hired as a consultant for one of those reality TV shows that transforms struggling businesses. His meeting was with several high-powered television executives. "It was the worst meeting ever," he said. "What a complete waste of time."

I asked him to elaborate on what happened.

"It all went wrong before it even began. No one was prepared. There was no set agenda, no objective, and no one had any idea of when their mission would be accomplished. That invited the 'idea fairy' to show up and a whole bunch of stupid ideas to surface."

The meeting wasted three hours and thousand of dollars in the time of those highly paid executives. This happens every day in all types of businesses and charities.

But the problems can be fixed. A little preparation, in terms of both the attendees and the planned outcome, will make a huge difference in your meetings and ultimately in the success of your day and your business.

Running meetings well is a skill and follows five simple steps taught to me by my business partner, Matt Smith, the publisher of Early to Rise.

Step #1 – Planning: Limit the Meeting to the Right People

The importance of having all the right people and none of the wrong people in the meeting cannot be overstated.

Every person in the room should be there for a specific reason. If you can't look around the room and explain very succinctly why each person is there then you're wasting someone's time and potentially everyone's time. Each person should contribute to specific decisions that are expected to be made OR take the action required after the meeting ends. Identify and eliminate the people who don't contribute to either of these causes. Having someone in the room to generate ideas isn't enough of a reason. Instead, consult with them before the meeting begins in your preparation.

Step #2 – Accountability: The Meeting Must Have a Very Clear Leader

The meeting leader is not an assumed role. It should be clearly stated in advance so the leader can properly prepare. The meeting leader must know what the primary activity is for the meeting in general and must drive forward the agenda. They must keep the meeting focused and moving. The purpose of a meeting can usually be boiled down to one (or a combination) of the four things below:

1. Making Decisions

2. Planning

3. Information sharing: One to Many

4. Information sharing: Brainstorming/Problem Solving

The meeting driver must know where they are in relation to the agenda, meeting objectives, and what activity would best serve that end at any point in the meeting.

Step #3 – Social Support: Stay Focused

In every meeting there will be times where the discussion will start to drift into side conversations that are irrelevant to the meeting objective. When this happens, the meeting leader must gently interrupt the conversation and bring everyone back to the decision you are trying to make. Everyone in the group should be mindful of this and contribute to keeping one another on track. Be gentle but firm, support one another, and respect one another's time.

Step #4 – Incentives: Have a Measurable Outcome (M/O)

Every meeting must have a stated measurable outcome. "By the end of this meeting we will have decided X, we'll appoint a driver to take responsibility for X, and we'll put together a rough timeline for when X will be launched."

It's a good idea to state the M/O before the meeting starts and at the end of the meeting make sure everyone agrees that the M/O has been accomplished. Be clear and concise.

For example: "We have a big proposal due at the end of this month. To complete this, we are going to break the proposal into categories and assign it to teams. So, the purpose of this meeting is to decide how we're going to delegate the work."

"The Measurable Objective for the meeting is this: By the end of the meeting we'll know exactly how we're going to break down the proposal. We'll decide on an approach to the proposal that we'll be presenting. We'll know what logistically is required to deliver the best proposal and we'll delegate specific tasks to teams to prepare the proposal."

Write the M/O on a flipchart or whiteboard where everyone sees it throughout the meeting. State the M/O at the beginning of the meeting to focus you and everyone else in the room on the goal of the meeting.

This will keep you on track and everyone will feel that it was a productive use of their time when at the end of the meeting they see the M/O was achieved.

Step #5 – The Big Deadline: End with a Plan and Give People Specific Assignments

Once decisions have been made, it's time to assign follow-up work to meeting members. Be specific. Make sure that each team member completely understands their objectives and can verbally restate them to the meeting driver along with the deadline for the delivery of the work.

Someone should write up a summary email that restates the tasks, owners, and due dates.

Having a clear and concise plan ensures the benefits of the meeting are not lost in the day-to-day shuffle of busy work. Only after this final step is the meeting truly wrapped up.

Efficiently planned meetings will respect everyone's time and propel the business forward. Start by having only the relevant team members attend the meeting. Be clear about the agenda and the measurable outcomes. Stay focused. Make decisions. Eliminate unnecessary conversations. Once decisions have been made, assign work specifically to individuals and get confirmation that they understand both their objectives and the deadline for their work. Don't leave unsettled decisions unless it cannot be avoided.

Follow that simple blueprint and you'll maximize your meeting time.

NINETEEN

THE PERFECT FOUNDATION FOR SUCCESS

Every successful person, no matter whether they realize it or not, has put the 5 Pillars of Success to work for them. They Plan and Prepare properly, they have Professional Accountability and Social Support, they have chosen an Incentive to inspire them, and they have given themselves a Big Deadline.

Remember what I said at the beginning of Part Two: If you have all 5 Pillars in place then you have the foundation to guarantee you will achieve your number one priority in life, whether it is to lose weight, make more money, or find the love of your life. But if one—or more—is missing, then your odds of success decrease dramatically.

If that's the case, and you are struggling, take heart and forgive

THE PERFECT FOUNDATION FOR SUCCESS · 117

yourself. It's not your fault. You just didn't know about the importance of the 5 Pillars until now.

"Be as kind to yourself as possible," Epictetus said. "Do not measure yourself against others or even against your ideal self. Forgive yourself over and over again. Then try to do better next time. Pursue the good ardently, but if your efforts fall short, accept the results and move on."

Basically, stop kicking yourself.

Everything ends at some point. Good times AND bad. Everyone goes through tough times but not quitting is what separates success from failure. You must persevere through the hard times knowing they will be over and you will get through them while savoring the good times.

We aren't perfect. We might fall back to bad behaviors, but the key is to use the 5 Pillars to pull yourself out of negative spirals and to get back to the right behaviors that will move you ahead to your goals. Mistakes are minor damage that can be dealt with. Look at every step forward as a small victory.

Fail forward, learn your lessons, move on, and remember that each second ticking away on the clock takes you further away from your mistakes of the past. You can't change them, but you can leave them behind. Don't dwell on the past. Focus on the future with the 5 Pillars.

Plan and prepare two solutions for every obstacle in life.

Find a coach or mentor to hold you accountable.

Get social support that will give you encouragement to get through tough times and that will kick your butt on days where you hold yourself back.

Give yourself a meaningful incentive that will inspire you to action.

And set a Big Deadline to put urgency into your action and keep you pushing to the finish line.

With the 5 Pillars in place, you will own the day, not regret the past. You will conquer the chaos of the afternoon even when the world around you is whipping itself into a frenzy. The 5 Pillars are the foundation of success. You can't move ahead without them. Take the time now to put them in place.

PART III

CONCENTRATE ON WHAT COUNTS

TWENTY

THE NEW LAW OF ATTRACTION

My story begins in 2001 when I first stumbled across Early-ToRise.com (ETR). It was exactly what I needed as a young, ambitious entrepreneur. Each morning when the ETR newsletter would arrive in my inbox, I'd stop whatever I was doing and read every word. The daily advice from my new virtual mentors—Michael Masterson, Yanik Silver, Dan Kennedy, and others—helped me grow my online fitness business to over seven figures in just a few years.

One day in 2005, I had an "a-ha" moment: *Why couldn't I be writing for Early to Rise?* After all, for the previous five years I had been a regular contributor to *Men's Health*, *Men's Fitness*, *Prevention*, and several other large fitness publications. And each day Early to Rise published a short health brief in their newsletter. It was the perfect fit. I tracked down the editor, made my case, and had my first ETR contribution published in November of 2005.

In March of 2006 I hired my first business mentor, Tom V. He helped me re-launch my online fitness program, Turbulence Training, which put me on the course to the financial independence I enjoy today. More importantly, Tom asked me one question that helped me achieve my dream.

At our first coaching session, Tom said to me, "Craig, what do you want your business to look like in five years?"

"I want to have a business like Early to Rise," I replied.

It was the first time I had revealed my dream with anyone, but it was clear in my mind. I wanted to give people the exact blueprint to success that would allow them to transform their lives physically, financially, mentally, and emotionally.

Sharing my dream with a mentor was the first step toward attracting good people and big opportunities into my life. It was a watershed moment. Still, there was a long road ahead— and a lot of work to do—before my dream would become a reality.

Two years later I met my future business partner, Matt Smith, in a Mastermind group. In October of 2010 Matt and I went on a testosterone-laden adventure trip with Yanik Silver and Tim Ferriss, racing cars and shooting guns in the Arizona desert with members of a real-life A-Team.

After the weekend, as Matt and I sat in the Tuscon airport waiting for our flights home, I told him my dream of building a business like Early to Rise. I wanted to reach a bigger audience than what was available through my fitness business. I wanted to help more people and change more lives. A few months later Matt and I started a website called www.InternetIndependence.com. It was a small but important step in the right direction.

Six months passed. On June 7th, 2011, I received a surprise email from Matt that asked, "If you could own part of and run ETR, would you?"

"Yes, of course," I said.

Matt was at a seminar with Mark Ford, the owner of ETR (Mark wrote the website's content under the pen name Michael Masterson). Mark told Matt that he was ready to sell the business and move on to a new venture. Seizing the opportunity, Matt and I flew down to Florida, met with Mark at his office in Delray Beach, and negotiated a deal. I had achieved my dream exactly five years, three months, and seventeen days since I first described it to Tom.

I had never experienced such a visceral actualization of my goals. Author Napoleon Hill's famous words rang true: "Whatever the mind can conceive and believe, it can achieve." It was a real-life example of the Law of Attraction at work, or something I more accurately call the Law of Action Attraction.

But as you can see I didn't just wish for Early to Rise and then wait for someone to give it to me. Instead, I worked hard, followed my rules, put the 5 Pillars in place, and concentrated on my vision every day. If you follow these steps, you too can achieve your big goals and dreams. Life is that simple. Success, freedom, and happiness will be yours with this blueprint in place.

First, you need to create the rules for your life. These keep you on the fast track to success and out of temptation.

The second step is implementing the 5 Pillars of Success. You need to plan and prepare to do the right things, you need a coach or mentor, you need to share your vision with positive people in your social support group, you need to give yourself an incentive for reaching your goals, and you need to have the big deadline for your actions.

Third, with your success foundation firmly in place, you need to create the vision for your life. A clear vision articulates exactly what matters to you. This is what you will concentrate on in life.

Every day you must take action that is congruent with your big goals and dreams. You must connect with positive, like-minded people to attract exactly what you want into your life. This works for finding love, building wealth, and improving your health. This success blueprint allows you to attain the life of your dreams.

TWENTY-ONE

HOW TO FOCUS ON WHAT REALLY, REALLY MATTERS

It might seem like I wrote this book backwards, leaving goal setting to the end, but I wanted to give you the formula for creating your Perfect Day before helping you write your vision for life. After all, it's no good to have big goals and dreams if you don't have the right tools and foundation in place to achieve them.

This is the payoff from adding structure into your life. You've earned the freedom to concentrate on what counts. What matters to you comes from your vision that you will create in this final section. It will strengthen your resolve to add more structure to your day. And from that you earn more freedom. It is a virtuous cycle.

According to life coach Tony Robbins, most people lose

momentum or get distracted when they don't have a vision. "We all need a compelling future, something that will get us up and excite us. If you don't have that, life feels very dead for high performers," he has said.

You may feel like there is a gap between where you are in life right now and where you want to be. This problem exists because you don't yet have a clear, defined vision for your life. Without this vision in place, your hard work is often misdirected toward unimportant goals that move you sideways in life rather than propelling you forward to your big goals and dreams.

Your vision also protects you from temptation. Every day you will be tempted to pursue the quick and easy reward and to sacrifice your future. Treats are fine, but let them remain just that.

What you choose to concentrate on at night is as important for your happiness and success as how well you choose to structure your days. Many people opt for short-term pleasure in binge-watching the latest popular television series. This is not unlike a child binge-eating Halloween candy. The rewards are immediate, but the remorse lasts longer. *Where did the time go*, you'll wonder, *and what good became of it?*

We must lose our desires to escape into fantasy, alcohol, and mindless pleasures each night. We must focus on being present, deeply present, with those around us who matter. You will always want more time to be with your family and friends, so use it. Don't look back and say, "Why did I watch so much TV?"

Look back and say, "I was truly there for their lives." Focus on what matters. Concentrate on what counts.

Having your vision will lift a tremendous burden from your shoulders. It keeps you focused and reminds you what is right for you in the long run and allows you to make decisions quickly and easily. You'll be amazed how quickly you can achieve your exact goals.

I first learned how to create my vision from Ari Weinzweig, CEO and cofounder of Zingerman's gourmet food company in Michigan. Over the years I've modified the exercise to help you be even more specific about what matters to you and to put in place the plan to achieve it. Here's what you need to do:

Step #1 – Write a First Draft

Creating your vision is not the same as goal setting. Crafting your vision requires writing as if you were living in the future, three to five years from now, and have already achieved your goals (see my example below). Knowing the end of the story will allow you to write the chapters that get you there.

Set aside an hour or two when you are most creative and free from distraction and write your vision without editing. Do not reject any ideas. Do not hold back. Create a big, bold, clear, concise, and specific vision.

Here's exactly how to get started. Answer the questions as if you were responding from the point in the future when your vision has been reached.

Start by identifying what you really want. Is it more money, or do you need more time, stronger relationships, or better health?

How do you measure success? (Be specific.)

What does your family and career look like? (Be big and bold.)

What does your family not do and what do you refuse to do in your career?

How do you feel about your family and career?

How do your family members feel about you and how do your peers feel about you at work?

What are the three most important things you offer your family and through your career?

What is your role in the family and in your career?

Who are you helping in your family and through your career?

What kind of people will you need to hire or connect with for your family or business?

What reputation does your family have and what reputation are you building at work?

What are the three most important accomplishments you want your family to achieve?

What are the three most important accomplishments you want to achieve in your career?

What is your mission in life?

What do you want your life's legacy to be?

Step #2 – Share Your Vision

Congratulations, you have created the first draft. Your next step is to share it with those who will help you achieve it. This means showing it to your spouse, your mentors, and anyone else who is both supportive of your vision and can provide meaningful feedback. Do not share your vision with those that will denigrate your efforts or dreams.

This is your treasure map. And you wouldn't share a treasure map with thieves that would steal your gold, so you must not share your vision with thieves that would steal your dreams. Ask your positive social support system for feedback. Take their recommendations and create a second draft.

If you do not have anyone who you can trust with your dreams, simply set aside your vision for at least twenty-four hours and then review it objectively. Question your decisions. Make sure you are creating your vision around what you truly want for your life, not what others want for you.

This exercise will give you tremendous clarity and optimism. It will give you a blueprint for success and it will right your sinking ship if you are struggling. This is the treasure map you've been looking for, and it was inside of you all along.

Step #3 – Re-Write the Final Version of Your Vision

Remember this: The vision for your life is to be written as your roadmap for success and to keep you on track. It prevents you from doing things that don't count, from worrying about what doesn't matter, and from trying to impress others. Your vision delivers you from evil and keeps you safe from harm. It is that powerful. You cannot have a rich and full life without it. You cannot win more freedom through structure in your day if it does not exist to guide you.

To help you create your vision, let me share the one I've written for my life.

The Ballantyne Family Vision

The year is 2020...TK and I have just celebrated our third wedding anniversary. Our two children, Jack (aged two) and baby Sophia, are the pride and joy of our lives and the center of attention as our families gathered at our home in Stratford, just ninety minutes from Toronto.

At our celebration we were surrounded with friends and TK's family, my sister and her family, and my mother. My business partners, Matt Smith, Bedros Keuilian, and Joel Marion, traveled with their families from America.

TK no longer works outside the home. She is a full-time mom

with help from our live-in nanny. I work from a home office and maintain strict business hours in a separate section of the house. I start work at 4 a.m. each day and finish at 4 p.m. so that we can have four hours of family time before bedtime. We eat dinner together every night at 5:30 p.m. I work a half-day on Saturday and Sunday is devoted entirely to family.

Matt and I operate Early To Rise (ETR), which is based in Denver. The business has grown to annual revenues of $20 million. We have certified over 2,000 personal trainers in our Turbulence Training program and this program contributes $3 million to our annual revenues. Jeff Schneider is our superstar COO and runs the day-to-day operations. My role is to speak at events, write content and create products, and inspire and encourage our employees through weekly coaching.

Five times per year I go on a weeklong work trip. Three days are spent in Denver at the ETR office followed with four days on the West Coast with Bedros where we coach over 1,000 entrepreneurs through our Mastermind meetings, seminars, and webinars.

TK and the children travel with me three times per year. In January we escape to our vacation home in Florida for four months. In the summer we visit Europe for three weeks where I teach at the annual BlackSmith Liberty and Entrepreneurship Camp in Lithuania. In late November we visit Florida for Thanksgiving with Joel Marion and family. That is followed with a trip to Denver for ETR's annual Toys for Tots charity drive.

Our biggest family ritual is holding a large celebration on Christmas Eve in our home in Stratford for all extended family and friends. Over one hundred people stop in on this magical night and we will continue with this incredible evening for the rest of our lives.

TK and I are heavily involved in local charities in our hometown community. We volunteer at the Stratford General Hospital and we also support the Stratford Slow Food movement and organic farmer's community. Each year we bring all three organizations together with a mid-December Christmas party for the families and to showcase the work of the food community.

Our number one priority is family. Our children mean the world to us and we look forward to the joys and challenges of raising them to be loving, compassionate, and responsible adults. We believe in experiences over material goods and that is why we accept the challenges of travel with our children, because we know the experience will be worth it.

TK and I are also committed to lifelong growth, both individually and in our relationship. We understand that we will evolve and we commit to being open to new experiences and constant learning. I love TK because she reminds me of what matters in life when my natural habit is to get caught up in trivial matters. TK supports me in my goal of writing five books. She has even committed to creating one of her own.

Our day-to-day life is simple yet abundant. We expect to be actively involved in our businesses and charity work well beyond the traditional retirement age of 65 years old. A good life is a virtuous life, we believe, one committed to helping others and sharing our good fortune and adding value where it will be valued in return.

The 3 most important things we can do for one another are:

1. Live by Example

2. Add Value

3. Give Love

Our friends admire our family and the more time they spend with us, the more they benefit. We encourage without preaching, we support without expecting anything in return, and we give to those who we know will give back in their own way. We are grateful every day for the life that we are able to live.

The End.

The Ballantyne family vision is not perfect. It will change. Unexpected twists and turns in life will happen. However, this vision gives us a clear direction to work toward. It allows us to build a roadmap that has a clear destination.

Your vision must inspire you, your family, your partners, and your employees (if you have them). Put your passion into it. Create your vision for what you want to accomplish, and act in congruence with it. Print it out. Keep it with you. Never waver. Use it to get through the tough times and dark days.

TWENTY-TWO

THE TRUTH ABOUT SETTING GOALS

With your vision in place, you can now go about setting specific outcomes and subsequent process goals to achieve them. Goal setting is not fantasy. It is about adding deadlines on your dreams, accepting ownership of your future, and identifying the actions you must take.

My mentor and the founder of ETR, Mark Ford, taught me that you should set only four goals at one time, one for your health, wealth, social self, and personal enrichment. These make up the key areas in a person's life. You are more likely to be a happy, well-rounded, and satisfied person when you are doing well in all of them.

By setting just one goal for these four areas you remain laser focused on what matters. If you set too many goals you end up without any priorities at all. Too many ambitious people make that mistake. I did for many years. But when I made the switch to Mark's system, success came faster, and I was less stressed. Even within these four areas, however, you are likely to be more focused on one area than on the others.

There's one more change you'll make to your goal-setting plan. The key to achieving your goals is to have the right steps in place to move you towards them. Without these steps in place, a lot of people lose momentum and quit pursuing their big goals and dreams. That's why you need to create several small process goals that will support the achievement of your outcome goals.

Most people focus only on outcome goals, such as "making $100,000 per year" or "losing twenty-five pounds." But these goals can be too big to comprehend, too abstract to achieve. The solution is to create process goals to go with each outcome goal so that you have a series of action steps that move you towards your big goal each day or week.

To perfect your goal-setting plan, you must a) determine what actions are needed to achieve that end result and subsequently b) go out and do it. By setting a clear outcome goal and creating three specific process goals to support it, you commit to doing everything in your power to turn your dreams into reality. For example, if you want to lose twenty-five pounds, adding process goals such as "I will do bodyweight workouts three times per week," "I will stop eating each night at 7 p.m.," and "I will walk 10,000 steps each day" puts you in a better position to succeed.

In a lot of ways, process goals are the most rewarding aspect of goal setting. They take any huge goal and break it down into an unintimidating series of actions, giving you a constant sense of accomplishment in the pursuit of your overall ambitions.

Here are more specific ideas to help you set your outcome and process goals for each of the four areas in life.

1. The Health Goal

Anybody who has ever experienced poor health knows just how vital good health is to productivity and happiness. Without good health, it can feel like nothing else matters. I understand this firsthand. In 2006 I struggled with crippling anxiety attacks for over six months. My anxiety was so strong that it kept me up at night and stopped me from pursuing many of my other goals. It was only through implementing the 5 Pillars of Success that I was able to overcome the anxiety and return to good health and to get back on track toward my other goals. That is why I understand the importance of continuing to set a health goal each year.

Even if you are fortunate to be in good health today, do not take it for granted. Don't ignore this area of your life until something bad happens.

When it comes to choosing a health goal, think about all the areas you could improve that would enrich your life. What specifically do you want to change? Do you want to improve your blood pressure, lower your cholesterol level, decrease your body weight, or reduce your body fat percentage?

Maybe your health goal is to stop doing something that is bad for you, such as smoking or drinking too much alcohol. Or, maybe your goal is to exercise regularly. And even if you are already doing most things right, you could probably benefit from eating more green vegetables, drinking more water, or getting more sleep. Choose one outcome goal to fix your biggest health concern and create three process goals to help you achieve it in ninety days or less.

2. The Wealth Goal

If you can meet your wealth goals, achieving your goals in all other areas of your life will become far easier.

Whatever your financial circumstances, be specific when setting your wealth goal. How much do you want to earn this year? How much do you want to reduce your debt? How much do you want to pay off of your mortgage?

Wealth goals can also include lifestyle-related changes. Decide which is the most important to you and which would you like to change first.

- Do you want to be able to afford to send your child to private school or college?
- Do you want to move to a different, more expensive, safer neighborhood?
- Do you want to save for a particular dream vacation?
- Do you want to buy something specific?
- Do you want to make a large charitable donation?

When setting process goals for wealth, try creating a three-account system. This system forces you to think about your money as being in three funds: your *expenses* account, your *savings* account, and your *investment* account. One of your wealth process goals will involve putting a system in place that automatically adds a certain amount of money to take care of each account every month. Adding money into each account will increase your wealth over time.

Break down your wealth goal into smaller steps and you will achieve progress every week, creating the momentum that will support you moving in the right direction.

3. The Social Self Goal

This category refers to your relationship with others, including your family, your friends, and your co-workers. What relationships are most important to you? How can you improve—or fix—them?

- Do you want to take your family on vacation?
- Do you want to meet a new life partner?
- Do you want to reconcile your relationship with a family member?
- Do you want to meet twenty new people in your community?
- Do you want to find a mentor?

If you are looking to meet new friends or find a life partner and you do not set goals, chances are you won't do anything about it. Much more likely, you will sit at home feeling lonely, wondering where you are going wrong. You need process goals to move you to action in the right direction. For example, one process goal would be to do three social outings per week, such as attending a basketball game with friends, joining a group that meets to play cards, volunteering on a community project, taking up dance lessons, etc.

You might be tempted to skip out on setting goals for improving your social self. Don't make that mistake. You will notice that each of your goals supports the others, and that the actions you take will get you closer to more than one of them. This is important as it reiterates just how central and inter-connected the actions you take are to your overall success in life.

4. The Personal Enrichment Goal

If you think of social self goals as working on the development of your outward facing self, then personal enrichment goals cover improvements you want to make within.

Do not leave out personal enrichment from the goal setting equation. It's easy to see why you set your other goals. You want to have wealth because money is helpful. It's a useful tool. It is better to have money than to not have money. Health is important because you cannot enjoy life without it. Your social self is important because you need a network of strong, healthy relationships. But equally as important, your personal enrichment goals allow you to enrich your mind and your soul...rewards that often prove to be the most satisfying. What is more, they can also be the most fun ones to work towards.

Make sure you choose something that is really worthwhile to you.

Examples of personal enrichment goals include a desire to speak a foreign language or to read every book on a list of classics.

You might focus on your creative side, finally writing the novel you had been putting off for years. You might set a goal to get involved in hands-on charity work rather than just donating money to a cause. You might choose a spiritual approach, reading books about religion or attending a retreat, delving deeper into prayer and/or meditation, or attending church every week.

If you want to deepen your understanding of and commitment to your religion, your process goals would be to sign up to attend a Bible study course and commit to attending every meeting. Another process goal would be to carve out time each week to review each lesson in advance. A third process goal would be to find a study buddy. With these in place, success is inevitable.

Experiences also lend themselves to solid personal enrichment goals. How often do you hear someone say, "I've always wanted to swim with dolphins," "I'd love to go to Japan," or "I'd like to do a parachute jump"? If that sounds like you, why not set a timeframe for the experience, and work towards all the things you need to do to make it happen?

The bottom line is that just about anything you would like

to do or improve about your inner self counts as a personal enrichment goal. Just remember, this goal is all about working towards things that are personally rewarding and which help make you, in your mind, a better person.

You now have four outcome goals and three process goals for each. With these in place you will build momentum every day, no matter how small of a step and now matter how big of a goal. You will begin to feel as though you can achieve anything.

We are not done yet though—there is still one more step you can take to make your goals even easier to achieve.

You have to share your goals if you want to get results. The trick is to only share your goals with the right people, those who will support and encourage you. I cannot emphasize enough how important it is to find the right people.

Who are the right people?

It may not be anyone you know right now. It might be that everyone around you is a source of frustration—negative people at work and at home. Clearly, this environment makes it difficult to share your goals. It will only lead to negative feedback.

But the right people are out there.

The Internet can help. You can find forums and Facebook groups for all interests. Simply look to join communities with people who will be interested and enthusiastic about your goals—you might even inspire some of them to set their own goals. It is incredible what you can accomplish when you get social support *and* when you *give* social support.

When you help other people, whether it's in a volunteer group or an online weight-loss forum, you gain as much benefit as the person you are helping. You will learn just as much as they will. So get out there, take those goals, and share them with the right people.

Take baby steps if you are uncomfortable sharing. It is okay to anonymously share your goals online. What you will most likely find is that not only does nothing bad happen, but good things happen when you do it. People—complete strangers— will support you. There are good people left in the world, trust me.

Once you get positive feedback and support, you will then start to think, *Okay, I'm going to share a little bit more now and maybe I'll be a little bit more accountable by including my name with it.* This grows your goal setting strength.

Not only does accountability allow people to help and support you (which they will want to do), but it also forces you to stick with your goals and take the right steps.

If you set a weight loss goal and share it with people at your gym, they will hold you accountable. In turn, you will not want to let them down, so you will make sure you attend every one of those gym sessions you said you would when you first set your process goals.

Sharing goals also provides you with a supporting cast who will want to celebrate your successes, from the smallest task you set yourself right through to those long-term outcome goals. Reaching a goal is often a long journey, and an impressive achievement. If you share it with the right people it will be even more rewarding when all that effort pays off.

The simple truth is that sharing your goals does not have to be intimidating. Seek out the right people, treading carefully if you are not ready to sit down and tell a friend or partner what you are doing. Look for other people who have similar goals and support each other. And celebrate every success—be proud of what you achieve and accountable for what you have said you will do. By following these simple principles you will stay motivated and disciplined, while achieving your goals far more quickly.

TWENTY-THREE

WHEN YOU SHOULD (AND SHOULDN'T) GIVE UP

Winston Churchill once told the people of Britain, "*Never give in—never, never, never, never, in nothing great or small, large or petty, never give in except to convictions of honor and good sense. Never yield to force; never yield to the apparently overwhelming might of the enemy.*"

There is but one thing missing from his advice. The key is to never, ever give up on what is *important to you.* There are some things that you can, and should, give up on. Some battles are meaningless and some wars are futile. Too many people have spent too much time fighting for things they don't really want or were only chasing because other people insisted that they do so. Even when you win those battles, you still lose because you have wasted valuable time.

The solution is to back up. Return to the exercise. Identify what really matters to you, not what matters to your parents, your co-workers, or society. Focus on your vision for your life. No one else has the exact same vision. Yes, you must weigh this against the responsibility you have for others in your life, such as your family (parents, partner, off-spring). But once you have your vision, then you have what is important to you, and that is where you must concentrate your energy.

Now you can heed ol' Winston's words. Now you can go forth, taking action, and never, ever giving up on what is important to you. It's full speed ahead, avoiding the negative people, attracting the positive, and reaching the big dreams and goals that you have set for your life. Once you accept the power of this big vision that you have generated, all of the small things that help you have Perfect Days become so much more important. When you are working towards a grand vision, you can't afford to waste time or sacrifice energy to other endeavors. As the old adage goes, "Life is not a dress rehearsal." This is our one shot. We must make the most of it.

The world will tempt us with fantasy football, breaking news, celebrity gossip, and television show marathons. These are not part of your vision. They do not move you closer to your goals. You must stay strong, controlling what you can, coping with what you can't, and concentrating on what counts.

TWENTY-FOUR

YOUR PERFECT DAY FORMULA REVEALED

I want to congratulate you on all that you have achieved so far in life and for your decision to step up, call yourself out, and take it to the next level.

As a high-performer, you've never been satisfied. Deep inside you've always harbored a nagging suspicion that you could achieve more, do more, win more, and earn more. You know you can have it all. You know it's possible. You've seen it done by others.

You know you've not reached the true greatness you are capable of. You know that you are destined for bigger and better things. You know there is a big breakthrough in your future. You can feel it. You know that you are only a few steps away from achieving your deepest desires. It's a feeling that you can't put into words, but it's there inside of you every day.

What you had been missing was the exact formula for getting there. Until today. Now you have the tools in place. You have your rules. You've set the foundation with your 5 Pillars of Success. And you have your vision to guide you.

With the Perfect Day formula you now have the map to the hidden treasure that is buried within.

It looks like this:

This proven success system has walked you through what really matters, motivating you to take action on the biggest priority in your life, helping you achieve your goals faster than ever, and showing you how to create automatic actions that get you big and bold results every day. It all starts with your magical fifteen minutes in the morning and grows from there.

It took me almost twenty years to put together this treasure map for you. It is worth more than a college degree or even a winning lottery ticket. It is proven by both science and experience, not just wishful thinking. Tens of thousands of people—just like you—have followed this map to success. This is your time. This is your turn.

Listen...

You're close. So close to making that big breakthrough.

You're ready to make the big leap and play up a level.

You just need to be pushed over the edge.

Your time is now.

Don't be frustrated by past struggles. They were simply there to get you where you are today.

In almost all areas of life—from losing weight to making money—we go through a long period of doing the work with minimal results...and then suddenly we experience a WHOOOOOOSH effect when the breakthrough occurs thanks to having the 5 Pillars of Success in place.

That's why you must continue to stick to your structured plans, to do the work, and to build the momentum. Take action every day. If you persist, nothing will stop you from making progress. You must never, ever give up on what is important to you.

In twelve months from now, you will be one year older. But if you also want to be better, then you must accept that your life is your personal responsibility. If you want to change, it is up to YOU and you alone. There are far too many people who have started in worst places than you who have gone on to make big changes for you to say that you can't do it. It's already been proven possible. Make the decision to change and take action today. Put your head down and do the work.

Begin at once a program of self-mastery. Stick with your

purpose. Do not seek external approval. Do not worry about anything outside of your control. Stop aspiring to be anyone other than your own best self.

"The sooner you set yourself to your spiritual program, the happier you will be," Epictetus said. "The longer you wait, the more you will be vulnerable to mediocrity and feel filled with shame and regret, because you know you are capable of better."

You success starts in the morning. Plan your day. Get up early. Work on your number one priority in life before anything else. Add more structure to your day and you will have more freedom in your life for your family, friends, and hobbies.

This is your one and only chance. Use the Three C formula today to own your days and experience the big WHOOOOOOSH you've been waiting for. You CAN do it. I believe in you.

You have uncovered an unstoppable success formula. Create your rules, set your foundation with the 5 Pillars, and write the vision for your life. These tools are your roadmap for success.

It's time for you to control your mornings, win your day, and achieve your big goals and dreams. Success starts with making the right decisions, right now, for your right life. Let's go!

ABOUT THE AUTHOR

CRAIG BALLANTYNE has been the Editor of the personal development newsletter, Early To Rise, since 2011. His daily essays reach over 150,000 readers and teach people how to build their wealth, improve their health, and become the best version of themselves. He now coaches entrepreneurs around the world how to turn their ideas into money and to help people all over the world.

Craig is also a fitness expert and the author of the groundbreaking fat loss workout systems, Turbulence Training, and Home Workout Revolution. He has been a contributing author to Men's Health magazine since 2000. He created the Turbulence Training Certification program to show personal trainers how to help men and women lose weight without equipment or cardio exercise. There are hundreds of TT Trainers around the world dedicated to his 10 Million Mission of helping ten million men and women transform their lives before 2020.

Craig has an advanced research background, completing a Master of Science Degree in Exercise Physiology from McMaster University in Hamilton, Ontario, Canada. He continues to study the latest in health and performance and to help his readers improve their lives. You can get Craig's daily advice for free at www.EarlytoRise.com and www.TTFatLoss.com.

– TWITTER @CRAIGBALLANTYNE